Praise for *Consuming the Word*

"In his latest book, Scott Hahn takes lessons from the Early Church to reveal the New Testament in a whole new light. *Consuming the Word* is essential reading for Catholics who want to better understand how the sacred authors and apostles affect us today."

—Matthew Kelly, author of *Rediscover Catholicism*

"*Consuming the Word* will increase your appetite for God and draw you into divine intimacy. Dr. Hahn brings clarity to the term "New Testament" as he moves us from text to action, from page to passion. Disciples of Christ have been called not to a text but to a covenant. The invitation to anyone studying the bible is to go deeper, to go beyond study to worship, to go beyond the words to the Word made flesh. For those who grasp the message of this book, their understanding of the Eucharistic sacrifice will never be the same."

—Jeff Cavins, author of *My Life on the Rock*

"Catholic scholars may debate certain details about how to understand Scripture, dogma, and liturgy, but all can agree that these three realities inseparably illuminate each other. Scott Hahn powerfully articulates these connections and their consequences for the love relationship into which the God of Love calls us."

—Matthew Levering, professor of theology, University of Dayton

"*Consuming the Word* reflects the strong connection between the authority of the scriptures and the authority of the Church. It will challenge anyone who gives it a fair hearing."

—John Michael Talbot, author of *The World Is My Cloister*

OTHER BOOKS BY SCOTT HAHN

The Lamb's Supper: The Mass as Heaven on Earth

Hail, Holy Queen: The Mother of God in the Word of God

First Comes Love: Finding Your Family in the Church and the Trinity

Lord, Have Mercy: The Healing Power of Confession

Swear to God: The Promise and Power of the Sacraments

Letter and Spirit: From Written Text to Living Word in the Liturgy

Reasons to Believe: How to Understand, Explain,
and Defend the Catholic Faith

Ordinary Work, Extraordinary Grace: My Spiritual Journey in Opus Dei

Signs of Life: 40 Catholic Customs and Their Biblical Roots

Many Are Called: Rediscovering the Glory of the Priesthood

Catholic Bible Dictionary, General Editor

Understanding the Scriptures: A Complete Course on Bible Study

Understanding "Our Father": Biblical Reflections on the Lord's Prayer

A Father Who Keeps His Promise: God's Covenant Love in Scripture

Covenant and Communion: The Biblical Theology of Pope Benedict XVI

Kinship by Covenant: A Canonical Approach to the
Fulfillment of God's Saving Promises

The Kingdom of God as Liturgical Empire: A Theological
Commentary on 1–2 Chronicles

Scripture Matters: Reading the Bible from the Heart of the Church

Spirit and Life: Interpreting the Bible in Ordinary Time

Rome Sweet Home: Our Journey to Catholicism (with Kimberly Hahn)

Living the Mysteries: A Guide for Unfinished Christians
(with Mike Aquilina)

Politicizing the Bible: The Roots of Historical Criticism and the
Secularization of Scripture (1300–1700) (with Ben Wiker)

CONSUMING

THE

WORD

THE NEW TESTAMENT AND THE EUCHARIST
IN THE EARLY CHURCH

Scott Hahn

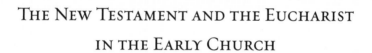

IMAGE
New York

Copyright © 2013 by Scott Hahn

All rights reserved.

Nihil Obstat: Reverend James Dunfee, Censor Librorum

Imprimatur: Most Reverend Jeffery Monforton, Bishop of Steubenville

The nihil obstat and imprimatur are official declarations that a book or
pamphlet is free of doctrinal error. No implication is contained therein
that those who have granted the nihil obstat and imprimatur agree
with the contents, opinions, or statements expressed.

Published in the United States by Image, an imprint of the Crown Publishing
Group, a division of Random House, Inc., New York.
www.crownpublishing.com

IMAGE is a registered trademark, and the "I" colophon is a trademark of
Random House, Inc.

Library of Congress Cataloging-in-Publication Data is available upon request.

ISBN 978-0-307-59081-7
eISBN 978-0-307-59082-4

Printed in the United States of America

Book design by Christine Welch

Jacket design by Laura Duffy

Jacket photography © Art Resource

1 3 5 7 9 10 8 6 4 2

First Edition

*To Timothy Cardinal Dolan, good shepherd
and pioneer of the New Evangelization*

CONTENTS

CONTENTS

FOREWORD

by Donald Cardinal Wuerl, Archbishop of Washington

Those who have been baptized into new life in Christ are also called to evangelize. Pope Paul VI reminded us that the Church exists to evangelize, and so Catholics cannot find fulfillment if they are not witnessing to the truth. More recent popes have called this task the "New Evangelization."

The New Evangelization is not a program. It is a mode of thinking, seeing, and acting. It is a lens through which we see the opportunities to proclaim the Gospel anew. It is the work of the Holy Spirit active in the Church.

The continuation of the mission of Christ, which began with the Great Commissioning following his death and Resurrection, is what we are engaged in today. The Acts of the Apostles tells us that as Jesus prepared to return to his Father in glory, he charged his disciples, "You will be my witnesses" (Acts 1:8). That same challenge echoes in our ears and hearts today—we are the witnesses to Jesus

Christ, his message, his way of life, his triumph over death, and his pledge of new life to all who would walk with him.

It is the task of the New Evangelization to bring the Word of God to the world. The Word of God is not a book. It is a divine person (see John 1:1). In Jesus, God has spoken and revealed himself. We receive that revelation, in its fullness, in the Scriptures and the sacred tradition preserved and announced by the Church.

Our proclamation is focused on Jesus, his Gospel, and his way. Christian life is defined by an encounter with Jesus. When our Lord first came among us, he offered a whole new way of living. The excitement spread as God's Son, who is also one of us, announced the coming of the kingdom. The invitation to discipleship and a place in the kingdom that he held out to those who heard him, he continues to offer today. This has been true for twenty centuries. As his message was more fully understood, it became evident that Jesus offers us not a new way of living but also a whole way of being.

The Church is the voice that transmits the Word to the world. Like John the Baptist, the Church cries in the wilderness that the Messiah has come. The New Evangelization calls us to render that voice intelligible to our age. The Word never changes, but the voice must be clear and relevant. The tone must be alive and enthusiastic. Our witness must be heard in the places where our people are.

In the Sermon on the Mount, Jesus addresses those who hunger and thirst for righteousness. Jesus's disciples are challenged to envision not only a world where the hungry are fed and the thirsty given drink, the stranger is welcomed and the naked are clothed, but also, and most amazingly, a world where sins are forgiven and eternal life is pledged.

That same vision is held out for us today when we open the pages of the Gospel and read about the invitation for us to eat the bread of everlasting life and to hear the words of truth, words that endure forever.

God is calling his Church to renew her efforts for the salvation of all. Just a few years ago I joined my brother bishops in Rome for a synod on the Word of God in the life and mission of the Church. Soon afterward we gathered again for a synod on the New Evangelization. The Church is seeking and finding creative ways of sharing the "words of eternal life" (John 6:69).

Pope Benedict XVI, in his apostolic exhortation *Verbum Domini*, wrote that "the primary setting for scriptural interpretation is the life of the Church" (n. 29). The Church is the home of the Word of God.

The Church urges us to read the Bible and to do so in the full context of centuries of reflection on its meaning under the guidance of the Holy Spirit. The study of the Bible by groups or individuals remains an occasion of God's continuous grace and enlightenment. This is why the Church so strongly urges that studying and praying from the Bible should be the lifelong project of every Christian.

It is precisely at the liturgy, however, that the vast majority of practicing Catholics regularly have a life-giving encounter with Jesus Christ. The liturgy is both an act of worship and a teacher of doctrine. The Bible is proclaimed abundantly at every Mass; and homilies give our clergy opportunity to explain and apply the Scriptures in light of tradition to the circumstances of everyday life.

Consuming the Word, by my good friend Dr. Scott Hahn, describes vividly the dynamic of the Word of God's inexhaustible power for shaping lives, families, societies, and civilizations. This he does in terms that are appealing for a broad ecumenical audience.

Anyone acquainted with the rich body of writing that flows so inspiringly from the hand and heart of Dr. Hahn knows he brings profound personal insight to his demonstrated theological expertise. *Consuming the Word* continues in that illustrious tradition. It brings us a powerful and welcome guide as we take our place in the great and challenging work in sharing the Good News. The Lord is accomplishing something great in our day. It is a privilege to be witnesses to it. *Consuming the Word* makes our task all the easier.

—*Cardinal Donald Wuerl*

TASTE AND SEE:
A PREFATORY WORD

In the years when I was educated, books were the conspicuous consumption of an intellectual. And by books I mean the paper product, bound between covers with its distinctive textures, colors, and aromas.

Not to be hidden under the bushel of an electronic device, they once lined floor-to-ceiling shelves in the homes of professors and authors. The spines were delectable in their variety of colors and stoutness.

My own consumption bordered on the gluttonous. In those years before online databases, I haunted library sales, yard sales, and garage sales. I sent off postcards alerting rare-book dealers to my "wants." When I traveled for business, I routinely spent my meal allowance on books, which I devoured in between meetings, on public transportation, in waiting rooms—wherever, whenever. I would forgo sleep to read still more.

My habits became the subject of good-natured jokes

in my extended family. When my in-laws sent me on an errand, they knew to allow time for my detours in bookshops. When we moved our household from Illinois to Ohio, the truckers had to take the weight of hundreds of crates of books into consideration and detour from the interstates in order to avoid fines for overload.

Consuming words, I had put on a bit of weight, and it showed. It still shows. Anyone who visits my house gets a tour of my library, which now includes tens of thousands of volumes shelved on an entire floor of a substantial home in Steubenville, Ohio.

Most of the books I own are books of theology, so most of the words I consume are words (*logoi*) about God (*Theos*). As I devoured these books by the hundreds, I found that they—curiously enough—pointed beyond themselves. They pointed to a meal.

Why should this have been strange to me? I knew that Jesus himself was a great devourer of books. He had been schooled in the Law, the Prophets, and the histories of ancient Israel; and even the day he rose from the dead he spent interpreting those books (see Luke 24:27). His "opening" of the Scriptures that day was a clear affirmation of the importance of the books, but it was nonetheless a prelude to his fuller self-revelation "in the breaking of the bread" (see Luke 24:30–35). At Emmaus the eyes of the disciples were finally opened as they sat at table with Jesus. At Emmaus Jesus fulfilled the words of the Psalm:

"Taste and see that the Lord is good!" (Psalm 34:8), following its sequence rather exactly.

In the early days of my book collecting and book consuming, while I was a new Catholic and a graduate student at Marquette University, I led a Bible study in my home. Most of the members were Catholic undergraduates who were unaware of the sacramental riches of their tradition. My wife, Kimberly, still Protestant at the time, complained that she and I had spent so much time studying the menu while these young people had been enjoying the meal.

Enjoying the meal, they were better equipped to appreciate the menu—once they understood the connection. That was as true of the young readers in my Bible study as it was of the disciples at Emmaus. Consuming the Word of God made them hunger ever more for the words of God.

So, to help people make the same connection, I have written yet another book, and I pray that it will be consumed with delight by many people. This book appears as a third course, as it were—a main course—following after my earlier titles *The Lamb's Supper* and *Letter and Spirit*.

It is not an academic book, though I hope scholars will find it satisfying and useful. Yet it is not quite a book for beach reading either. Some of the material is demanding, though I hope I have placed it well within reach of motivated lay readers.

Some years ago I founded the St. Paul Center for Biblical Theology. Its mission is twofold: to promote biblical literacy for Catholic laypeople and biblical fluency for Catholic scholars and clergy. This is the second book I have written with the hope of reaching both audiences with a common message.

"A man once gave a great banquet, and invited many; and at the time for the banquet he sent his servant to say to those who had been invited, 'Come; for all is now ready'" (Luke 14:16–18).

✝

CHAPTER I

The Sacrament of the Scroll

An ancient tradition tells us the story of Saint Romanus the Melodist, the sixth-century composer of homilies in hymn form, and how he received his vocation.

Born in Syria, he was a reverent child who loved the Lord's house. Early in life he entered the service of the Church, at first simply lighting the lamps and preparing the incense for worship. As he grew, he pursued his education in Beirut, where he was ordained a deacon.

Romanus was the sort of student who got good grades because his teachers recognized the earnestness of his efforts. He was zealous, and his zeal enabled him to do good things in spite of mediocre skills. After three years in Beirut, he moved on to serve the Church in the imperial capital, Constantinople.

He was humble enough to recognize his shortcomings, and he accepted them. In fact, he took the word "lowly" as a sort of personal title. He longed, however, to glorify God as did the deacons who were better singers. Music was such an important part of divine worship, especially in the Eastern churches. It pained Romanus that the musical quality of the services he led was so inferior to that of the services led by his colleagues.

He prayed for God to give him by grace what he lacked by nature and training. One night as he prayed he fell asleep and was visited in a dream by the Virgin Mary. She held out a scroll to him and bid him, "Take the paper and eat it." He did as he was told. He ate the scroll. Then he awoke and immediately knew what he must do.

He dressed and ran to the church. Ascending to the pulpit, he began to sing a sermon on the birth of Jesus. The song he sang is today known as his masterpiece—one of more than a thousand verse homilies (*kontakia*) he composed in his remaining years. A millennium and a half later, they are still sung on the great feasts of the Church.

::

Consuming the Word. Even casual readers may recognize Saint Romanus's apparition as a trope, or common figure, of mystical literature. In the archetypal instance, the prophet Ezekiel (2:9–3:4) reports a similar encounter with a mighty angel:

> And when I looked, behold, a hand was stretched out to me, and, lo, a written scroll was in it; and he spread it before me; and it had writing on the front and on

the back, and there were written on it words of lam-
entation and mourning and woe. And he said to me,
"Son of man, eat what is offered to you; eat this scroll,
and go, speak to the house of Israel." So I opened my
mouth, and he gave me the scroll to eat. And he said
to me, "Son of man, eat this scroll that I give you and
fill your stomach with it." Then I ate it; and it was in
my mouth as sweet as honey. And he said to me, "Son
of man, go, get you to the house of Israel, and speak
with my words to them."

The story recurs in the New Testament, in John the
Seer's encounter with a "mighty angel" come down from
heaven, "wrapped in a cloud, with a rainbow over his
head," his face "like the sun, and his legs like pillars of
fire" (Revelation 10:1f).

He had a little scroll open in his hand... I went to the
angel and told him to give me the little scroll; and he
said to me, "Take it and eat; it will be bitter to your
stomach, but sweet as honey in your mouth." And I
took the little scroll from the hand of the angel and
ate it; it was sweet as honey in my mouth, but when I
had eaten it my stomach was made bitter. And I was
told, "You must again prophesy about many peoples
and nations and tongues and kings."

It is an odd sort of episode, the eating of a book, and
it is all the more fascinating because it occurs in not one

but two biblical texts. No wonder it commanded the attention of so many of the earliest Christian commentators. By the time of his own apparition, around AD 518, Romanus, who lived in a monastic community, must have heard the works of the great interpreters read aloud many times. He could have little doubt about the meaning of his dream.

Saint Hippolytus of Rome, in the third century, was one of the earliest exegetes to produce extended commentaries. He wrote that the scroll, with its printing on front and back, "signifies the prophets and the apostles. In it the Old Covenant was written on one side and the New on the other." Moreover, the scroll symbolizes the "secret, spiritual teaching... There is a connection between reading the outside and understanding the inside." There is a connection between the Old and New Covenants, and only the one who consumes the scroll can see it.

For Saint Jerome, the Ezekiel passage contained a special message for preachers: "Unless we eat the open book first, we cannot teach the children of Israel."

In the generation after Romanus, Saint Gregory the Great experienced the same fascination, returning repeatedly to the prophet's text. Gregory, a pope and liturgical reformer, was a profound exegete. In his *Commentary on Ezekiel* he wrote: "What the Old Testament promised, the New Testament made visible. What the former announces in a hidden way, the latter openly proclaims as present. Therefore the Old Testament is a prophecy of the New Testament; and the best commentary on the Old Testament is the New Testament."

For the Fathers—from Hippolytus and Jerome to Romanus and Gregory—the meaning was abundantly clear: Salvation comes by means of a covenant (also known by the Latin equivalent, "testament," from *testamentum*); and the covenant must be consumed so that it can be shared.

::

To Catholic Christians, in the first century or the twenty-first, the mystical tropes always evoke the sacramental mysteries. In the instances I've discussed so far, it is no stretch. The visionary books of Ezekiel and John are rich with liturgical imagery. Ezekiel is much concerned with the Temple. John sees both heaven and history in terms of sacrificial liturgy: altars and priests, chalices and censers, trumpets and hymnody, culminating in a sacred banquet. In both cases, the consumption of the scroll takes place amid some experience of heavenly worship.

In John's telling, and later in the Church's account of Romanus's life, there are Eucharistic overtones. Both men are invited to "take" and "eat," two verbs familiar from the Eucharistic institution narratives since the first century (see, for example, Matthew 26:26). They receive the covenant *verbally*, and they take and eat that "word" as food.

In the third century, Origen, the great teacher of Alexandria, spoke of the scriptural proclamation as analogous to the sacramental communion:

You who are accustomed to attending the divine mysteries know how, when you receive the body of the Lord, you guard it with all care and reverence lest any small part should fall from it, lest any piece of the consecrated gift be lost. For you believe yourself guilty, and rightly so, if anything falls from there through your negligence. But if you are so careful to preserve his body, and rightly so, why do you think that there is less guilt to have neglected God's word than to have neglected his body?

For Origen, there is a sacramental quality to the scroll. It is to be handled and consumed with the same decorum and attentiveness—yet hungry eagerness—as the Eucharistic bread.

In the bread and in the word there is a real presence. In the proclamation and in the sacrament the kingdom arrives with the king himself. Pope Benedict XVI wrote, "Thus we grow in the realization, so clear to the Fathers of the Church, that the proclamation of the word has as its content the Kingdom of God (cf. Mark 1:14–15), which, in the memorable phrase of Origen, *is the very person of Jesus (Autobasileia).*"

This is the truth Romanus knew, and Jerome, and Gregory, and John experienced, and Ezekiel foresaw. Salvation comes by way of a covenant—a covenant embodied in a Word, a Word that is made flesh, a Word that is consumed.

The prophets and seers speak to us in images, and their images convey mysteries. As we come to understand these mysteries, we must use words to speak of them. God made us to communicate verbally. He himself created this aspect of human nature and accommodated it as he inspired the Scriptures—which are, literally, *hai graphai*, "the writings." For Ezekiel and for John, God committed his word to a scroll before inviting them to consume it.

God reveals himself and gives himself in the scroll. What begins as poetry, however, we can allow to degenerate into jargon; and so the Greco-Latinate terms "covenant," "testament," "liturgy," and "Eucharist"—all workaday words that inspired our ancestors to sing—now drop with the thud of a technical vocabulary.

It is probably not a modern problem, but rather a perennial temptation. Yet our recovery of the *newness* of that vocabulary—the *New* Testament, the *New* Covenant—is especially urgent right now, as the Church embarks upon a *New* Evangelization.

Evangelization is a dynamic process by which we share the Gospel (the Good *News*) with others. Yet we cannot deliver what we do not first possess. Ezekiel consumed the word of his prophetic message. John, too, took it and ate it. Romanus consumed it, digested it, and it became part of him; and then he shared what he had received. These men first knew communion with the Word, and only then were they able to take the Word out to the world.

We all need to sense once again the savor of Ezekiel's

foretaste, John's banquet, Romanus's song. That is the reason I wrote this book: to undertake a study of a few of Christianity's most basic terms, and to find out what they meant to the sacred authors, the apostolic preachers, and their first hearers. If we consume the Word as they intended when they served the Word, then we can be transformed as the early disciples were transformed, and then perhaps our world can be remade and renewed as theirs was remade and renewed.

CHAPTER 2

✚

Before the Book

If someone asks about the basics of Christianity, the foundations of our faith, we instinctively draw from literary terms. We speak of the "New Testament," and by that we mean a book. We point to the "Gospel," and by that we mean a literary form, a kind of sacred biography. We use these terms as titles of specific ancient documents, texts that were composed millennia ago and fixed permanently by a "canon," which we understand to be an unchangeable table of contents.

"New Testament" is indeed a foundational term. Today, it's most commonly used to describe the second division of the Christian Bible, the later-written and smaller division, which consists of twenty-seven books. All of those individual books were written after the earthly ministry of Jesus, and they reflect upon that ministry and its implications for humanity. "New Testament," then, is a book title, and it belongs to Christianity's most sacred and authoritative text.

If "New Testament" is a title, then it's only sensible that modern Christians use literary terms to talk about it. But here's the problem: We have no evidence that anyone in the first century used the term that way. In fact, we don't find "New Testament" applied to the Christian Scriptures until the very end of the second century; and only in the middle of the third century does the term appear with some degree of frequency. We do find it early on, but it does not refer to a written work. In fact, it has quite a different meaning, which we'll get to in a moment.

Yet even when authors did get around to calling the book by that name, they didn't always agree on which texts belong in the book. Although there was widespread agreement about the four Gospels, the Acts of the Apostles, and most of Saint Paul's letters, there was a bit of contention about the so-called Catholic Epistles, attributed to Peter, James, and John, about the Letter to the Hebrews, and about the book of Revelation. There was, moreover, a handful of books that were considered "Scripture" in some local churches but not in others: the first-century letters attributed to Barnabas and Clement, for example, and the visionary book called *The Shepherd*, by Hermas of Rome. Not until the fourth century do we find a "canon" with exactly the same list of books as you'll find in today's Christian Bible.

The faith of the first-generation Christians was centered on something they called the "New Testament," although ordinary believers and even the Church's leaders had only limited exposure to the sacred texts. They did not have the benefit of a fixed canon. Few people had access to books anyway.

We all agree that the life of those early Christians is somehow exemplary and normative for Christians today. If we are to succeed in the Church's New Evangelization, it will be at least partly because we follow the pattern of the first evangelization. The love of Christ compels us to understand their terminology on *their* terms.

::

To understand the mind of the earliest Christians we need to exercise our imagination, for we're talking about a time before the advent of mass media. There were no electronic or instantaneous communications—nothing like television, radio, podcasts, e-mail, or the World Wide Web. Ordinary postal mail could take months to reach its destination.

Neither was there a printing press. Book production was laborious. Scribes—who were skilled, highly paid professionals—spent hours copying out legible pages by hand with pen and ink. Just one copy of a book could require a month to complete. Only the very wealthy could afford to own such volumes, and usually no more than a few. In most places, moreover, education was available only to the elites. Literacy levels in the Greco-Roman world were relatively low, so there was not a large ready market for books. It's probably safe to say that the early Christians could not have imagined a world where the Bible was waiting in a drawer in every hotel bedroom or was mechanically searchable in a pocket electronic device.

Nevertheless, we find—from the very beginning—a profound reverence for the sacred writings: *graphai* in Greek, usually translated to English as "Scriptures." Most of the time when the word is used in the New Testament books, it refers to the books of the Old Testament. That's how Jesus uses the term when he says, "the scriptures… bear witness to me" (John 5:39). That's how Saint Luke uses the term when he says that "beginning with Moses and all the prophets, [Jesus] interpreted to [his companions on the road to Emmaus] in all the scriptures the things concerning himself" (Luke 24:27).

Yet the first-century authors seem to indicate that the writings of their own generation also were Scriptures—that they were *sacred*—and sacred in precisely the same sense that Israel's Law and Prophets were. Long before there was a biblical canon, we find the Second Letter of Peter referring to the writings of Saint Paul as *graphai*, "Scriptures," just like the "other scriptures," the sacred books of Israel (see 2 Peter 3:16). The practice is not restricted to the canonical books but is evident also in first-century works attributed to Barnabas and Clement of

Rome; both cite the Gospel of Matthew as "Scripture." Early in the second century, Saint Polycarp of Smyrna refers to the Psalms and to Saint Paul's Letter to the Ephesians together as "these Scriptures."

It is clear that the primitive Church revered certain texts, produced in living memory, as sacred and authoritative. Such reverence was reserved for documents that could be traced, in some way, back to one of the Apostles of Jesus Christ. Thus, the Gospels of Matthew and John enjoyed privileged status because both Matthew and John were numbered among the Twelve. The Gospels of Mark and Luke were honored because they were associated with Peter and Paul, respectively, and were composed by the closest disciples of these men.

By the middle of the second century, it was clear that those four Gospels—and only those four—represented the reliable account of the earthly deeds of Jesus Christ. Writing in Rome around AD 155, Saint Justin Martyr emphasized the Gospels' historical character as eyewitness documents; he calls them "the memoirs of the Apostles." To Saint Irenaeus of Lyons, writing around 170, the four Gospels were as firmly fixed as the four points of the compass. "The Gospels," he says, "could not possibly be either more or less in number than they are."

The evangelical scholar Larry Hurtado proposes another, very practical reason for the fourfold collection. He believes that the "collection of Gospels... embodies a diversity of voices and contents." Though the Gospels were composed in different places for a variety of purposes, there was a general consensus about their apostolic origin. Gathering the four together, Hurtado concludes, was "an early and deliberately 'ecumenical' move," representing an "effort to express and affirm a certain diversity or breadth in what is treated as authoritative."

The new Christian Scriptures were preserved, treasured, honored, and circulated universally. They belonged not to one or another Christian community, but to what Saint Ignatius of Antioch, already in AD 107, called *he katholike ekklesia*, that is, the universal Church, the Catholic Church.

Recent biblical scholarship makes a strong case that the texts were treated as sacred, and thus inviolable, from a very early date. Nothing else could account for the relatively few variations in the early copies that have survived. Scribes were simply not permitted to "improve" John's grammar or Paul's style. When copying the apostolic texts, scribes were restricted in a way they were not when they copied the letters of Saint Ignatius of Antioch or the apologies of Saint Justin Martyr.

There was widespread consensus regarding these Scriptures, yet there was no official canon imposed by any official act of any centralized authority. Indeed, even the word "canon" held a different meaning for those first generations than it does for us today. Though the early Christians frequently used the Greek word *kanon*—which can mean "measuring stick" or "list"—it was not until the fourth century that they applied the term specifically to the list of biblical books.

For the early Christians, "canon" was a term that encompassed all of Christian tradition. The Greek Fathers referred to *kanon tes aletheias* (the canon of truth) while their Latin contemporaries spoke of *regula fidei* (the rule of faith). The term encompassed the Church's faith in its entirety—the Scriptures, yes, but also the rituals, customs, order, and disciplines handed on by the Apostles.

So we see that the notion of a canon preceded the official designation of "the canon" by centuries. Similarly, the concept of "the Gospel" preceded the designation of four literary artifacts as "the Gospels." In the beginning the Gospel is simply "Good News" (Greek, *euangelion*), and Jesus himself embodies it. Mark portrays Jesus inaugurating his ministry by "preaching the gospel of God," which Jesus summarizes as follows: "The time is fulfilled, and the kingdom of God is at hand" (Mark 1:14–15). Jesus exhorts his listeners to "repent, and believe in the Gospel" that he has just announced.

The content of the Gospel is quite simply Jesus. He represents a fulfillment and a kingdom. He *is* the Gospel long before the literary Gospels were written. He himself *is* the canon long before the official canon came into being. Christians preached this Good News and proclaimed it and lived it out long before anyone wrote a word of it down on parchment or papyrus.

::

If we seek to understand the vocabulary of our faith as the early Christians understood it, we must be willing to be surprised. What the basic terms mean today in common parlance they did not necessarily mean in the Church's first generation. Indeed, they could not mean the same thing. Christians could not share a universal literary culture when they could not easily share documents. What they shared instead was the "news," the "message," and their "canon" was the basic outline of that proclamation.

The Good News was to be a New Testament, based on the term that Jesus himself had employed. But what did he mean by it? And what's so *new* about the testament he came to establish?

Again, our inquiry takes us back to our earliest sources. Again, we should expect to be surprised.

CHAPTER 3

✟

The New Testament in the New Testament

N ew Testament" appears six times in the documents that were eventually brought together as
the biblical New Testament. Six times might
not seem like a lot, but they were significant. What did
the first Christians mean by this term? What did Jesus
mean the one time he used it? Since there was no book by
that name, both Jesus and his early followers must have
meant something else. But what?

The word we render as "testament" is, in Greek, *diathēkē*.
In the early Greek translation of the Jewish Scriptures
(called the Septuagint), *diathēkē* is used as the equivalent
of the Hebrew word *berith*. Both *diathēkē* and *berith* may be
rendered more accurately in English as "covenant" rather
than as "testament." In ancient cultures, both words denoted "a widespread legal means by which the duties and
privileges of kinship may be extended to another individual or group." To the Jews of Jesus's time, a covenant

created a family bond where none had existed before. Marriage was considered a covenant, as was adoption.

A covenant was normally marked by a solemn ritual oath, sealed with a blood sacrifice and, often, with a shared meal. The resulting kinship entailed obligations and prohibitions, which were sometimes detailed in writing. Blessings were pronounced upon those who kept the covenant, and disciplinary curses upon those who violated its particular law. The original term, the Hebrew *berith,* was used to describe relations between two human parties as well as the bond between God and his people. God enacted covenants with Noah, for example, with Abraham, and with Moses.

Berith was sometimes even used to describe the ritual oath by which parties entered or renewed a covenant. Thus, we read of "the covenant of circumcision" (Acts 7:8). The ritual was so important to parties of a covenant that it served as a shorthand term for their personal and collective identity. Thus, Saint Paul could refer to his fellow Jews as simply "the circumcision" (Colossians 4:11).

Berith was also sometimes used to denote the wider complex of relations, acts, laws, and institutions that a covenant entailed—the new order it brought about for those who entered the relationship. *Berith* was even identified with specific elements of the covenantal relationship. The Law of Moses, for example, could be called simply "the book of the covenant" (Exodus 24:7; see also Sirach 24:23 and I Maccabees 1:57).

::

The term "new covenant" first appears in the oracles of the books Christians later came to know as the Old Covenant, and it appears only once: "Behold, the days are coming, says the Lord, when I will make a new covenant with the house of Israel and the house of Judah" (Jeremiah 31:31). The prophet Jeremiah speaks of a *berith chadasha* (rendered in the Greek Septuagint as *diathēkē kainē*)—a "new covenant." Jeremiah's oracle is the obvious precedent for the several appearances of the term in the Gospels and Epistles.

In the apostolic documents the phrase appears five times with some form of *kainē diathēkē*: Luke 22:20; 1 Corinthians 11:25; 2 Corinthians 3:6; Hebrews 8:8, 13; and Hebrews 9:15. (In Hebrews 12:24, we find a similar phrase, *diathēkē nea,* which is also rendered as "new covenant.")

Jeremiah's oracle had foretold a new familial relationship, but recognizably in continuity with the old. The covenant would be "new," but God would make it within the Old Covenant's structures: the houses of Israel and Judah. It would be like the Old Covenant in that it would involve law, kinship, and blessings. But it would also be "not like" the old (see Jeremiah 31:32), because it would be everlasting and would remain unbroken. Thus we see its newness, expressed once with the Greek word *nea,* denoting recency in time, but overwhelmingly with the Greek word *kainē. Kainē* expresses a quality in this covenant that is different from anything that has gone before—a quality of freshness and permanence. The same adjective is used to describe Jesus's "new commandment" (John 13:34) and his creation of "a new heaven and a new earth" (Revelation 21:1). These are things that remain "new" even thousands of years after they first appeared on the scene.

How, then, do we explain the preponderance of the English term "New Testament" rather than "New Covenant"? The distinction appears only in Western translations, which have been influenced by the Old Latin and the Vulgate. Seeking an equivalent for *berith/diathēkē* in Roman culture, Latin-speakers found nothing exact and settled on the Latin word *testamentum*, a word often associated with bequests: "my last will and testament." Thus, ancient testaments often take the form of farewell discourses delivered by Israel's father figures (e.g., Jacob, Moses, Joshua, Jesus). Facing death, these men gathered their sons, tribes, or disciples (typically twelve) to renew the covenant and impart future blessings for their 'family' (see Genesis 49; Deuteronomy 33; Joshua 23–24; John 14–17). Other examples of testamentary literature can be found among the Dead Sea Scrolls and elsewhere. A testament is a final statement of one's lasting moral legacy. In that sense, *testamentum* was the best of the available options in Latin. The documents of the apostolic generation accomplished that much, and so the word "testament" took its place in the Scriptures and the liturgies of the West.

Still, it is inexact; for in the culture that extended from Jeremiah to Jesus a covenant accomplished more than any testament could. In fact, a covenant *was* that culture. It was the bond that constituted Israel's law, liturgy, and life.

::

In all of Jesus's sayings, we find just one instance when he used the phrase we translate as "New Testament," and he used it to describe neither a will nor a book, but rather a sacramental bond.

Saint Paul provides the earliest historical record of the event, perhaps twenty years after the fact, in his First Letter to the Corinthians: "In the same way [Jesus] also [took] the cup, after supper, saying, 'This cup is *the new covenant* [*hē kainē diathēkē*] in my blood. Do this, as often as you drink it, in remembrance of me'" (1 Corinthians 11:25, my italics).

What Jesus is doing, and commanding those present to "do...in remembrance," is obviously very important. His words convey the deepest solemnity, and he speaks them in the gravest context: the ritual sacrificial meal of the Passover, at the beginning of his sacred Passion.

The event was clearly important to the early Church as well. The account of this offering of bread and wine occurs in all three synoptic Gospels as well as in that letter of Saint Paul. The association of the cup with "the covenant" occurs in Saint Luke's Gospel (22:20), just as it does in Paul's Epistle.

These passages clearly mark the ritual event that inaugurated the "New Testament." Jesus equated the particular event—and even its elements, its vessels—with the New Testament.

Jesus's words evoke the oracle of Jeremiah (31:31), but also the account of Moses's ratification at Sinai of Israel's covenant with God. There Moses extended the covenant to the people by ritually sprinkling them with the blood of sacrificial animals: "Behold the blood of the covenant which the Lord has made with you" (Exodus 24:8).

Jesus's action, like Moses's, inaugurated a covenant, and did so with the offering of a blood sacrifice shared with those in the covenant family. Thus, in Jesus's only use of the term, we find that "New Testament" refers not to a text, but to a rite and to the new order brought about by means of that rite.

Use of the term in the Epistles confirms this association. The term "new testament/covenant" appears repeatedly in the context of a discussion of liturgy or priestly service and mediation—the ministry of Jesus or the ministry of the Church.

From Saint Paul we learn that God has made Paul and other Apostles "competent to be ministers of a new covenant" (2 Corinthians 3:6). The word "ministers" is, in the original, *diakonous*, "deacons," which, in Greek as in English—and for first-century Christians as well as first-century Jews—is the title of a liturgical office, a sacred ministry (see 1 Timothy 3:8–13).

In the Letter to the Hebrews, we find two references to the "new testament/covenant," both occurring in chap-

ter 8's discussion of the transfer of the sacrificial priesthood. Later in the same letter, we read of Christ as the
"mediator of a new covenant" (9:15 and 12:24); he is the
mediating priest whose "sprinkled blood…speaks more
graciously than the blood of Abel." Dense with sacrificial
imagery, the line may well be a reference to the Church's
Eucharistic liturgy, the "assembly [*ekklesía*, "church"] of the
first-born" who have gathered at "Mount Zion" (a prob-
able allusion to the traditional site of Jesus's Last Supper)
"in the city of the living God, the heavenly Jerusalem"
with "innumerable angels in festal gathering."

Thus, when the phrase "new testament/covenant" appears in the *document* now known as the New Testament,
it appears consistently amid the discussion of sacrificial
liturgy and priestly office. The covenant is equated with
its ritual sign and is administered by men who hold cultic
office by divine appointment.

::

The language with which the biblical New Testament
speaks of the "New Testament" bespeaks a certain sacrificial character. Sacrifice is the primary function of priesthood, after all. As noted earlier, the New Testament, like
the Old, was ratified with the shedding of blood. Thus,
Jesus invoked Moses's "sprinkling" with blood as does the
Letter to the Hebrews.

Jesus's death was the once-for-all sacrifice (Romans
6:10 and 1 Peter 3:18), the singular, unrepeatable sacrifice
of the New Covenant. All Christians in every age have

agreed upon this point. But it is useful for us to ask why this is so. What made Jesus's crucifixion a sacrifice?

To those formed by millennia of Christian tradition, the idea seems self-evident. But to a first-century Jew it would have seemed unthinkable. Sacrifice was permitted in only one city, the holy city, Jerusalem; yet Jesus was crucified outside the city walls. Sacrifice could be offered in only one place in that holy city, in the Temple, on the altar, by a priest from the tribe of Levi; yet Calvary was a hill far from the Temple, and it had no altar and no offering priest.

To even the most careful observer, the crucifixion of Jesus would have appeared to be a profane event, a fairly unremarkable Roman execution. A sympathetic soul might have judged Jesus's death to be an act of martyrdom, like the deaths recounted in the histories of Maccabees (see 2 Maccabees 7), but not a sacrifice.

Some years ago, Joseph Ratzinger (the future Pope Benedict XVI) made a similar observation.

> How could it ever occur to anyone to interpret the Cross of Jesus in such a way as to see it as actually effecting what had been intended by the cults of the world, especially by that of the Old Testament, by what had often been dreadfully distorted in them and had never been truly achieved? What opened up the possibility at all of such a tremendous rework-

ing of this event, of transferring the whole of the Old Testament's theology of worship and the cult to this apparently most profane occurrence? . . . Jesus himself had told the disciples about his death and had interpreted it in terms of prophetic categories.

What made Good Friday's death a sacrifice, then, was the offering Jesus had made—in explicitly sacrificial terms, during his Last Supper with his disciples. There he made an offering of "body" and "blood." He declared it to be his "memorial," a term (in Greek, *anamnesis*; in Hebrew, *zikkaron*) associated with the Temple's sacrificial liturgy. And he identified his action in terms of prophetic categories, most explicitly the "new covenant" of Jeremiah's oracle.

For Ratzinger, this detail of the biblical record is the key to the Church's theology of the Eucharist:

> *the interpretation of Christ's death on the Cross in terms of the cult* . . . represents *the inner presupposition of all Eucharistic theology* . . . An event that was in itself profane, the execution of a man by the most cruel and horrible method available, is described as a cosmic liturgy, as tearing open the closed-up heavens—as the act by which everything that had hitherto been ultimately intended, which had been sought in vain, by all forms of worship, now in the end actually comes about.

It is, moreover, what makes the New Testament what it is: "Here, with unique clarity, we encounter *what is specific to the New Testament*, what makes it new in comparison with the previous covenant history, which thus becomes the Old Testament."

In the text of the New Testament, then, "New Testament" denotes not a text, but an action—not a document, but a sacrament.

✠

CHAPTER 4

The New Testament After the New Testament

The New Testament's understanding of the term "New Testament" is confirmed, at least implicitly, by the way Christian writers employed the term in the two and a half centuries following the generation of the Apostles.

The Fathers of the Church are those teachers from antiquity whose "witness" is treasured by Christian tradition. To the meaning of the New Covenant, they provide a witness that is coherent and consistent with what we have seen so far in the documents of the apostolic generation.

It is important to note, however, that outside the Scriptures the phrase "new testament/covenant" appears *nowhere* until the middle of the second century. What we find instead are occasional references that implicitly present two dispensations, both dependent on a particular covenant with God.

This is abundantly clear, very early on, in the first-century Letter of Barnabas. Attributed to the Apostle and companion of Saint Paul, the document enjoyed a measure of authority in the early Church. In its pages, the covenant emerges as a recurring theme, and the author frequently employs the word *diathēkē*. Though he never uses the phrase "New Covenant/Testament," he does speak of "the covenant of the beloved Jesus" in contradistinction to the covenant of Moses. Thus he *implies* that there is an "old" as well as a "new" (as Saint Paul also does in 2 Corinthians 3:14).

Similarly, in the late second century, Saint Melito, bishop of Sardis (Sart in modern Turkey), wrote to a man named Onesimos who had inquired after a list of the trustworthy books. Melito provides a roster of what he calls "the books of the Old Covenant." Once again, though he does not mention a "New Testament," the mention of an "old" seems to imply the existence of a "new."

Writing sometime around the 170s, Saint Irenaeus, bishop of Lyons, uses the phrase "new covenant" in several places in his book *Against the Heresies*, most extensively in book 4, chapter 34, where he refutes the claims of the Marcionites on the one hand and the Jews on the other. The arch-heretic Marcion, who lived at the same time as Irenaeus, argued that the Jewish Scriptures had never been valid and that the god of Moses was a cruel tyrant and not the supreme God. The Jews, for their part, rejected the Christians' claim that Christ had fulfilled the covenant with Israel because he established a new covenant that included the gentiles along with ethnic Israel.

For Irenaeus, "New Covenant/Testament" refers to the dispensation, the cosmic order, brought about through Christ's sacrifice. He does not explicitly connect the covenant with the liturgical act, except by quoting the Gospel account of the Last Supper. We should recall, however, that it was Irenaeus who taught that the Christian worldview—the Church's distinctive understanding of the new world order—is utterly dependent on the liturgy of the New Covenant: "Our way of thinking is attuned to the Eucharist," he writes, "and the Eucharist in turn confirms our way of thinking."

In the next decade, Saint Clement of Alexandria, head of the famous Egyptian catechetical school, wrote about the "New Covenant/Testament" not only as a dispensation, but also as essentially related to liturgical worship. Christ "made a New Covenant with us; for what belonged to the Greeks and Jews is old. But we, who worship him in a new way, in the third form, are Christians. For clearly, as I think, he showed that the one and only God was known by the Greeks in a Gentile way, by the Jews Judaically, and in a new and spiritual way by us."

Elsewhere, Clement made it plain that the New Testament is, in its essence, the sacrament of the Eucharist. Comparing Christian life to an athletic competition, he wrote that each believer should "go and submit himself to the Word as his trainer, with Christ as the referee of the game; and for his prescribed food and drink let him have the New Testament of the Lord."

Later, most movingly, Clement declared that the sacrament of the New Testament is the reason God became man in Jesus Christ: "For this he came down. For this he clothed himself in humanity...And just before he poured out his offering, when he gave himself up for a ransom, he left for us a New Testament: 'I give you my love' (see John 13:34). What is that love and how great is it? For each of us he gave his life, the life which was worth the whole universe, and he requires us to do the same for each other."

So far we have traced usage of the term "New Testament" to the end of the second century. We have invoked witnesses from lands as far-flung as Turkey, Egypt, and France. And we have found the use of the term to be coherent and consistent. Orthodox scholar Father Theodore Stylianopoulos aptly summarizes our history to this point: "The expressions 'Old Testament' and 'New Testament' were not applied to the sacred books until the end of the second century. For the Apostle Paul and the early Christians the 'new covenant' was neither a book nor a collection of books, but rather the dynamic reality of the new bond between God and Christian believers based on the person and saving work of Christ."

⠿

As the second century turned over to the third, we find the first clear references to the New Testament as a limited and authoritative collection of texts, and we find an increased usage of the Latin word *testamentum*. Our great witness at this point is Tertullian, a North African and a lawyer by training, who favored legal terminology even as he practiced theology. His background in law may indeed explain his frequent use of the Latin word *instrumentum* (a legal document) to describe the collection of apostolic texts. Yet he also employed *testamentum* to denote the collection of biblical books. At least once he used both terms, *instrumentum* and *testamentum*, seemingly interchangeably in the same sentence. Sometimes, too, he referred to the apostolic writings as "the Newest Testament" (*novissimum testamentum*). His fluid use of terms suggests that the collection's title had not yet been firmly established for Latin-speaking Christians.

The collection itself, however, was authoritative. Tertullian applied his skills at argument against the Christian heresies emerging in his time, and it is from the biblical books that he marshaled his evidence. He argues against one opponent by using texts "out of the New Testament" as "a confirmation of our view."

By the middle of the third century, we encounter Church Fathers renowned specifically for their work of exegesis and biblical theology. The greatest of these, Origen, writing in Greek, routinely used "Old Covenant" and "New Covenant" to refer to the two collections of biblical texts. Saint Hippolytus of Rome, also writing in Greek, referred to "the two covenants"; and Saint Cyprian of Carthage wrote in Latin of "the Scriptures, old and new."

The works of the Church Fathers seem to indicate that the use of "New Covenant/Testament" *as the title of a collection* emerges only with the turn of the third century. Until that time, Christians identified the term "New Testament" primarily with a family bond—their relationship with God—and the resulting cosmic dispensation. This use of the phrase was dependent, however, upon *the ritual worship* Jesus had established in the offering of his body and blood. Church Fathers were dependent upon the Eucharist.

⠶

What we find in all the Fathers, from the beginning, is the strong use of covenantal language to describe the Eucharist, the rite Jesus referred to as "the new covenant in my blood."

Scripture scholars such as George Mendenhall have demonstrated that the rite Jesus established for the Eucharist was based on older traditional forms of a covenant oath. Mendenhall demonstrates that the account of Jesus's Last Supper in 1 Corinthians (and in Luke's Gospel) "presumes archaic patterns of thought and behavior that have been unattested now for several millennia. But these patterns were apparently known to Jesus, his disciples, and the early church, suggesting that the Eucharistic meal of bread/body and wine/blood in 'remembrance' of Jesus was itself the oath of a (new) covenant that was then being made." Jesus identifies himself with the offering, and he calls it his memorial sacrifice. Thus he uses the language of a covenant meal, covenant oath, and covenant sacrifice—patterns that were known to the early Church, which was composed mostly of Jews. This is the key to understanding the language the early Church used to describe the Eucharist. Its vocabulary was explicitly "sacrificial" in character; and this, according to Mendenhall, makes it implicitly covenantal.

Saint Ignatius, bishop of Antioch, wrote seven letters around AD 107 as he was taken by military escort to his execution in Rome. Addressed to churches along his route, they are neither treatises nor essays, but rather exhortations. He urges Christians to be unified, obedient, and strong in the face of persecution. He assumes a common Eucharistic practice, shared by all the churches, and a common Eucharistic doctrine. He employs a complex sacrificial vocabulary when he speaks about liturgical matters. He repeatedly calls the Church the *thusiastērion*, which is Greek for "altar" or "sanctuary"—literally, it is the "place of sacrifice."

Nor is Ignatius the first to apply such terms to the liturgy and its ministers. Preceding him by at least a decade (and perhaps much more) is Saint Clement of Rome, a pope of the first century. He asserts that the bishop's work is to offer the oblation (*prospheretia*).

An anonymous first-century document titled *The Didache* (or *Teaching of the Twelve Apostles*) also speaks of the

Eucharist as "the sacrifice" (chapter 14) and invokes the oracle of the prophet Malachi as its witness: "For from the rising of the sun to its setting my name is great among the nations, and in every place incense is offered to my name, and a pure offering; for my name is great among the nations, says the Lord of hosts" (Malachi 1:11). This is the prophecy most often applied to the Eucharist by the early Fathers. It is employed by Saint Justin Martyr, Origen, Saint John Chrysostom, Saint Augustine, and Saint John Damascus—and it is profoundly sacrificial in character. Recent scholarship suggests that the ritual sections of *The Didache* may even predate the Gospels themselves.

For the earliest Fathers, the Eucharist was simply "the sacrifice," the Church's sacrifice. No one put this in more lapidary terms than Eusebius of Caesarea, the bishop and historian of the late third and early fourth centuries. In the years immediately before the Council of Nicaea (AD 325), he composed his *Proof of the Gospel*, in which he considered the Eucharist as it is foreshadowed in the Old Covenant and fulfilled in the New. He writes: "We sacrifice, therefore, to Almighty God a sacrifice of praise. We sacrifice the divine and holy and sacred offering. We sacrifice anew, according to the New Covenant, the pure sacrifice."

The Eucharist was the sacrificial rite required by the covenant—and by the very *nature* of covenant. In the earliest documents of Christianity, the authors presume that the Church's ministers exercise a sacrificial office. They could assume this rather than assert it, because they could count on the understanding of the members of their churches.

For typical Christians of the twenty-first century, however, this may require some getting used to. As Mendenhall notes, the account of the institution of the Eucharist depends upon "archaic" thought patterns that have been "unattested" now for millennia. The rite of the New Testament depends upon the Old Testament. Simply stated: Most of us are unfamiliar with the practices and day-to-day life of first-century Jews in Palestine.

If these patterns have been "unattested," it is because Christians have had to translate the Gospel for cultures unfamiliar with Israel's institutions and social structures. This is the process Christianity has followed in all its efforts at enculturation. It is a necessary process, but it comes, sometimes, at a price. For the sake of understanding, we translate unfamiliar and ancient concepts into our own categories. *Diathēkē* is divided into three words in Latin: *testamentum*, which can mean "will"; *foedus*, which means "alliance"; and *pactum*, which usually means "treaty." Thus it takes three words to do the job that one accomplished in the original context of the Scriptures.

Nevertheless, even very early in Christian history, we find ample evidence that the Church understood the Eucharist to be the setting of a covenant oath. Around AD 111, the pagan governor of Bithynia, Pliny the Younger reported to the emperor Trajan that the Christians' Sunday worship consisted of the consumption of ordinary food and the swearing of an oath. The word he uses for "oath" is *sacramentum*, from which we get "sacrament." It is a word that will recur often in the writings of the Latin Fathers.

In Latin, the new dispensation was increasingly associated with the *testamentum*, or "will," and the term applied to the rite as well as, eventually, the Church's Scriptures. In the earliest Latin liturgies, the rite is called "*calix... novae et aeterni testamenti*" ("the cup of the new and eternal testament"). It is termed a "will," yet it is understood to be a covenant oath, a *sacramentum*. The New Testament could not be contained by the conceptual categories of the gentile world.

Throughout the age of the Fathers, the Eucharistic liturgy was consistently and universally known as "the sacrifice," and that in itself is incomprehensible apart from the biblical understanding of covenant.

::

This may sound remote, theoretical, and academic—an exercise in semantics. But to the early Christians it was not. It was the substance of their new life in Christ. If it seems like mere wordplay to us, perhaps it's because we have lost the primary sense of Christianity's most important words.

Consider Saint Cyril of Jerusalem preaching in the fourth century. He was addressing new converts to Christianity, men and women who had just been baptized as

adults. Like Saint Paul before him (see 1 Corinthians 8),
Saint Cyril contrasts the sacrificial meal of the Christians with the ritual feasts of the pagans. In the baptismal promises, he explains, the New Christians "renounce
Satan, breaking all covenant with him, that ancient league
with hell." He describes the pacts that had been made
with Satan as *diathēkē*, the word we translate as "testament" and "covenant"; yet he identifies them with ritual
actions: "idol festivals," where "meat or bread or other
such things are polluted by the invocation of the unclean
spirits, are reckoned with the pomp of the devil." The new
Christians had broken those former covenants with hell
as they entered the New Covenant, which he calls "the
paradise of God."

Lest you think this is all ancient history, consider a conversation with an African bishop who was recently visiting a friend of mine. He said the greatest problem facing
his Church was not poverty, not disease, and not hunger—
though his diocese struggled with all of these—but rather
"the covenants that our people make with demons."

The bishop's native language, unlike English, does
not introduce distinctions where none exist in the Bible.
So he sees a "testament" for what it is, and he knows the
power of the New Testament to overthrow all other testaments. In other words, he knows the New Testament as
the Apostles and the Church Fathers knew it.

He said that the most important new project in his

diocese was the establishment of a house where people could go to be released—through the power of the Gospel and the sacraments—from the pacts they had made with demons.

Such liberation from evil, he explained, can only happen through the power of the New Testament, rightly understood.

✙

CHAPTER 5

The Original Setting of the New Testament

W hat the first Christians knew as the "New Testament" was not a book, but the Eucharist. In a cultic setting, at a solemn sacrificial banquet, Jesus made an offering of his "body" and "blood." He used traditional sacrificial language. He spoke of the action as his memorial. He told those who attended to repeat the action they had witnessed: "*Do* this in remembrance of me" (Luke 22:19). Thus he instituted the Christian priesthood and established the Church's liturgy. He authorized clergy to *do* what he was doing: to make a memorial offering of his body and blood.

He called his action the "new covenant in my blood" (Luke 22:20). He declared it to be the New Testament— and the Testament was not a text but an action. He did not say "*read* this" or "*write* this," but rather "*do* this." By the time the Gospels and Epistles were written, the Church had already been faithful to Jesus's instruction for decades. The New Testament was a sacrament at least a generation before it was a document. We learn this from the document itself.

It was in the Upper Room, where the Last Supper was celebrated, that the Apostles received the outpouring of the Holy Spirit on Pentecost (Acts 2). From there they brought the New Testament to the world, celebrating it everywhere they went. Not even half of the Apostles wrote books; some of them probably did not live long enough to read any of the Gospels; but all of them went forth and offered the Eucharist, as Jesus had commanded them.

When at last the books were written, they described a Church already well established, with a developed ritual life. Indeed, it was in the midst of the Church's liturgy that the first Christian congregations encountered the Scriptures of the Old Testament. It was for proclamation in the liturgy that the books of the New Testament were written.

Even then, however, those books were not known as the New Testament. The documents weren't complete till the end of the first century, and even then they were not called the "New Testament" till the end of the second century. The documents only gradually took that name, again because of their liturgical proximity to the covenant sacrifice, the Eucharist. They were the *only* books approved to be read in the Eucharistic liturgy, and they were "canonized" for that very reason. Thus, precisely *as liturgical books*, they were called the New Testament.

::

The sacrifice offered at the Last Supper was consummated on the cross. The sacrifice that took place "once for all" was extended to all peoples, through all subsequent time, by its re-presentation in the Eucharist. The early Christians found this movement traced in the letters of Saint Paul. In his First Letter to the Corinthians, after introducing the "word of the cross" (1:18), he calls Christ "our paschal lamb" who "has been sacrificed" (5:7). Thus he makes the connection between the Passover celebrated as the Last Supper and the crucifixion on Calvary.

Indeed, it was Jesus's action at the Last Supper that transformed his death from an execution to an offering. At the Last Supper he gave his body to be broken, his blood to be poured out, on the "altar" of the cross. The Last Supper was the necessary first act in the drama of the Passion. It was like an opera's overture that established all the important themes that would recur and then resolve in the end.

As Paul retold the story of the Last Supper (1 Corinthians 11:23–25), he spoke of the event in sacrificial terms. He quoted Jesus's echoing of the long-ago words and action of Moses. He recounted that Jesus had called the Supper a "remembrance." Earlier, he had compared and contrasted the Christian Supper (the Mass) with the sacrifices of the Temple (1 Corinthians 10:18) and even with pagan sacrifices (1 Corinthians 10:19–21). All sacrifices, Paul said, bring about a communion, a fellowship. The offerings of idolatry bring about a communion with demons, but the Christian sacrifice brings about a communion (participation) with the body and blood of Jesus (1 Corinthians 10:16).

Thus, Jesus's death on Calvary was not simply a brutal and bloody execution. Jesus's death was transformed by his self-offering in the Upper Room. It became the offering of an unblemished Paschal victim—the self-offering of a high priest who gave *himself* as a victim for the redemption of others—the offering of a New Covenant, the New Testament. "Christ loved us and gave himself up for us, a fragrant offering and sacrifice to God" (Ephesians 5:2).

The Eucharist infused that love into the Church, uniting the Christians' love with Christ's love, the Church's sacrifice with his own. Saint Paul preached: "I appeal to you therefore, brethren, by the mercies of God, to present your bodies as a living sacrifice, holy and acceptable to God, which is your spiritual worship" (Romans 12:1). Note that he speaks of "bodies" in the plural, but "sacrifice" in the singular. For Christians are many, but the Church's sacrifice is one. It is united with Jesus's sacrifice, which is once for all.

This is what Jesus willed when he made his offering and then commanded his Apostles to repeat the action as his memorial sacrifice: "Do this in remembrance of me" (1 Corinthians 11:24–25).

:::

The document we call the New Testament presents the rite called the New Testament as something central to Christian belief and life. Redemption, as Christ accomplished it, makes little sense apart from his Eucharistic offering. Salvation, as Christ accomplished it, makes little sense apart from his Eucharistic offering.

The *only* significant narrative overlap between the Gospels and the letters attributed to Saint Paul is the institution narrative. Though Paul was Jesus's most prolific interpreter, he rarely quoted the Master. Yet here he carefully narrated the scene and reported Jesus's words at length. It is by far the longest quotation of Jesus's teaching found in the Pauline corpus. The Apostle emphasized that he himself is not the origin of the tradition. He is simply passing on what has already been well established in the Church. "For I received from the Lord what I also delivered to you, that the Lord Jesus on the night when he was betrayed took bread…" (1 Corinthians 11:23).

How well established was this tradition? The Acts of the Apostles conveys the worship of Paul's predecessors in a compact statement: "they devoted themselves to the teaching of the apostles and to the communal life, to the breaking of the bread and to the prayers" (Acts 2:42; cf. Acts 20:6–7). The Church in every succeeding age observed those four elements in its celebration of the Eucharist.

There are many other "Eucharistic" scenes in the New Testament, less explicit, perhaps, but no less vivid. Consider Saint Luke's account of Jesus's Resurrection appearance to the two disciples on the road to Emmaus. Jesus walked with them, but they did not recognize him. Then, "When he was at table with them, he took the bread and blessed, and broke it, and gave it to them. And their eyes were opened and they recognized him; and he vanished out of their sight... he was known to them in the breaking of the bread" (Luke 24:30–35). Saint Luke could hardly be clearer in connecting this event with the supper recounted two chapters earlier. Jesus's actions are almost identical; they reprise the theme introduced in the overture and bring his Passion to a fitting resolution. From the era of the Fathers onward, Luke's Emmaus account would become paradigmatic for Eucharistic theology: the opening up of the Scriptures that culminates in the breaking of the bread.

Saint John's Gospel presents the subject theologically in the Bread of Life Discourse (chapter 6), but also dramatically and symbolically in the same chapter as it tells the story of Jesus's multiplication of loaves. The Fathers of the Church believed that Jesus's act of transubstantiation at Cana—changing water to wine—was a symbolic foreshadowing of the Mass.

The Eucharist, instituted on the night Jesus was betrayed, appears in the Gospels as the Savior's first order of business when he rose from the dead. In Acts and the Epistles, it appears as the Church's constant concern as Christianity spread outward from Jerusalem to the whole world.

##

The New Testament as a document presumes and depends upon the New Testament sacrifice and the New Testament meal. Over the last fifty years and more, many Protestant biblical scholars have noted what Abbot Denis Farkasfalvy has called "the Eucharistic provenance of the New Testament."

What these scholars recognize is that the *documents* we call the New Testament were written to be proclaimed in the context of the *sacrament* we call the New Testament. They are to be "read aloud" in the assembly (Revelation 1:3). Thus, they use terms that were ordinarily, in the ancient world, associated with priesthood, sacrifice, and liturgy. They contain hymns and doxologies and sudden insertions of ritual formulas. These are sometimes lost on us, like the original meaning of "New Testament" itself, because we have covered them over with centuries of interpretation, translation, and homiletic use. But the forms would have been apparent to the original audience and the original authors.

Saint Paul opens his First Letter to the Thessalonians by assuring his hearers, "We give thanks to God always for you all, constantly mentioning you in our prayers"

(1 Thessalonians 1:2). The verb he uses for "give thanks" is *eucharistoumen*. Similarly, the First Letter to Timothy prescribes the offering of *eucharistias*, which is often translated as "thanksgiving." This usage certainly evokes Jesus's thanksgivings whenever he broke bread. The Gospels present him consistently "giving thanks," and to this end they use forms of the verb *eucharisto*. See Matthew 15:36; Mark 14:23; Luke 22:17; and John 6:11 and 6:23.

In Jesus's own milieu, these terms of "thanksgiving" could refer not only to generic categories of prayer, but also to a specific form of sacrifice. In the sacrificial system of the Jerusalem Temple, perhaps the most common rite was the *todah*, a sacrifice of bread and wine offered in thanksgiving to the Lord. Jews in the Greek-speaking world sometimes translated *todah* as *eucharistia*. That is how the word is rendered in the translation of Hebrew Scripture by Aquila, the second-century convert to Judaism and disciple of Rabbi Akiba.

To first- and second-century readers, the terms *todah* and *eucharistia* could suggest something more than polite expressions of gratitude. They had important sacrificial connotations for both Jews and Christians. More than a century after the fall of the Temple, the Midrash records the rabbinic belief that in the age of the Messiah "all sacrifices will cease except the *todah* sacrifice. This will never cease in all eternity."

Did Saint Paul intend his "eucharistic" terms to be read in a sacrificial sense? We cannot know for sure, but we should be open to the possibility. Recent research has made academic readers more sensitive to liturgical forms embedded in the Epistles. To first-century authors and their audiences, such forms would have been incomprehensible apart from some sense of sacrifice. A closer examination of the New Testament documents might incline us to find still more of the New Testament *sacrament* inside.

CHAPTER 6

✛

The Church of the New Testament

Jesus never wrote a book, a treatise, a poem, or an instruction. In the Gospels, the only time we see him writing, he "wrote with his finger on the ground" (John 8:6, 8), and we have no clear notion of what he wrote.

Instead of broadcasting his message in books, he proclaimed it by means of preaching and ritual action, and he appointed men who would do the same in perpetuity. As far as we know, he never told his chosen Twelve to write anything, though he did tell them to preside over his memorial sacrifice (Luke 22:19); and he told them to preach, baptize, and make disciples (Matthew 28:19). The Apostles, for their part, followed the lead of their master. Fewer than half of them wrote anything that survived the first century. The others, as far as we know, wrote nothing at all. The Twelve occupied a privileged place in Jesus's ministry, yet more than half of the New Testament was written by men who were not counted among the Twelve.

What Jesus and the Apostles did was not a work of publishing. What they did was establish a Church, with Jesus's appointed ministers as foundation stones (see Matthew 16:18 and Revelation 21:14). The proclamation of the Gospel presupposes not the activity of scribes, but rather the institution of a community—a communion.

Saint Paul put the matter in terms of necessity: "For, 'every one who calls upon the name of the Lord will be saved.' But how are men to call upon him in whom they have not believed? And how are they to believe in him of whom they have never heard? And how are they to hear without a preacher? And how can men preach unless they are sent?" (Romans 10:13–15).

Saint Paul, like the Twelve, proclaimed the Gospel without the benefit of the Gospels. He did so by means of public preaching and the Eucharistic liturgy, and this could not have happened apart from a preexisting Church with duly appointed ministers. It was through the Church that God did the calling, sending, and preaching. It was in the Church that Jesus's New Testament was ratified by means of a sacrifice—and a sacrifice always requires an officiating priest.

This was the rule of biblical religion, and it would always be the norm for the Church. Thus, Jesus himself was intensely interested in succession—the transmission of the Good News and the handing on of the New Testament. The process was not about texts and institutions so much as about persons. The Apostles proclaimed the Gospel and "handed on" the rites. That "handing on" is the root of the Greek word *paradosis* and the Latin *traditio*, from which we derive the English word "tradition." We have mentioned baptism and the Eucharist among the rituals they passed along. We might add anointing (e.g., James 5:14), confession of sins (e.g., John 20:23), and ordination (e.g., Acts 13:3). When Saint Paul relayed creedal and doctrinal material, he was careful to emphasize that "I delivered to you...what I also received" (1 Corinthians 15:3; 11:23).

The theologian Joseph Ratzinger (later Pope Benedict XVI) emphasized this "personal" element of the New Testament, noting that tradition is always linked with the notion of succession. In Christianity, he wrote, tradition is "never a simple and anonymous handing on of teaching, but is linked to a person, is a living word, that has its concrete reality in faith." Apostolic tradition and apostolic succession "define each other," he added. "The succession is the form of the tradition, and the tradition is the content of the succession."

[S]uccession is never the taking over of some official powers that are then at the disposal of the office-bearer; rather, it is being taken into the service of the word, the office of testifying to something with which

one has been entrusted and which stands above its
bearer, so that he fades into the background behind
the thing he has taken over and is...just a voice that
enables the word to be heard aloud in the world.

This process, Ratzinger noted, gives "the living word
of proclamation a superior status to mere Scripture," and
that itself "is a genuinely New Testament trait." As Saint
Paul put it: "So then, brethren, stand firm and hold to the
traditions which you were taught by us, either by word of
mouth or by letter" (2 Thessalonians 2:15).

It is not that Scripture has somehow been demoted. It
is rather that the New Testament subordinates the document to the sacrament. For the former depends upon the
latter. Saint Paul clearly speaks of his priestly ministry in
such terms, emphasizing that God "has made us competent to be ministers of a new covenant not in a written
code but in the Spirit; for the written code kills, but the
Spirit gives life" (2 Corinthians 3:6). He has been called
for service, not to a text, but to the covenant, which is
vivified by the Spirit through the sacraments that Christ
entrusted to the Church.

Succession is an interpersonal exchange. Paul has been
"*entrusted* with the Gospel." That is his watchword (see Galatians 2:7; 1 Thessalonians 2:4; 1 Timothy 1:11). Though
God initiated the mission, it was enacted in the Church,
when the elders examined Paul and then laid hands on
him (Acts 13:3). Paul begat his own successors in the

same way, by the same rite of ordination, with the same results: "I remind you to rekindle the gift of God that is within you through the laying on of my hands... Follow the pattern of the sound words which you have heard from me...; guard the truth that has been entrusted to you by the Holy Spirit" (2 Timothy 1:6, 13-14). Through the grace of ordination, Timothy has been empowered to preside over the Church's worship: "Till I come, attend to the public reading of scripture, to preaching, to teaching. Do not neglect the gift you have, which was given you by prophetic utterance when the council of elders laid their hands upon you" (1 Timothy 4:13–14).

Timothy is commanded, in turn, to follow his master even in the practice of ensuring succession: "and what you have heard from me before many witnesses entrust to faithful men who will be able to teach others also" (2 Timothy 2:2).

Paul handed on what he had received. This was as true of his ministry as it was of his Gospel. Paul viewed his office in terms commonly used for the sacrificial service of the Jerusalem Temple. He was "a minister of Christ Jesus to the Gentiles in the priestly service of the gospel of God, so that the offering of the Gentiles may be acceptable, sanctified by the Holy Spirit" (Romans 15:16). He describes a ministry that is unmistakably liturgical and sacrificial. In the "spiritual worship" of the New Testament, Christians present their "bodies as a living sacrifice, holy and acceptable to God" (Romans 12:1), and these are united in Holy Communion with the "once for all" sacrifice of Jesus Christ.

::

This concern for succession and tradition, which we find in the canonical Scriptures, is taken up in turn by the men who were appointed by the Apostles.

Saint Clement of Rome was, according to ancient tradition, a disciple of Peter and Paul. In the latter half of the first century, he served as a presbyter and then as bishop of Rome. It was Clement who set down the order of succession as he had received it: "The Apostles received the gospel for us from the Lord Jesus Christ: Jesus the Christ was sent from God. Thus Christ is from God, the Apostles from Christ. In both cases the process was orderly and derived from the will of God.... They preached everywhere in country and town and appointed their first-fruits, after proving them by the Holy Spirit, to be bishops and deacons."

Clement observes the tradition and succession because they are consonant with God's supernatural will; he observes, however, that they produce the natural benefits of peace and good order in the Church's earthly society. "The Apostles knew...that there would be contention over the bishop's office. So, for this reason...they appointed the aforesaid persons and made further provision that if they should die, other tested men should succeed to their liturgical ministry."

We find in Clement no novel teachings, but rather a

synthesis of the relevant doctrines of his master, Saint Paul. Saint Ignatius of Antioch, writing a few years later, is of the same mind. A bishop himself, Ignatius is intensely concerned about order, office, and authority. He wrote seven letters as he made his way to martyrdom in Rome, addressing six to local churches and one to a fellow bishop. In each he assumes that the local Church observes the apostolic order in the structure of its hierarchy: bishop, priest, and deacon. He assumes that the life of every Church is centered on the Eucharist. Like Clement, Ignatius may have had only a limited knowledge of the books that would eventually be compiled as the New Testament, but he had no doubt about possessing the Gospel of the New Testament. He had it from the Apostles. He had it in the Catholic Church and its sacraments, especially the sacrament of the New Testament, the Eucharist. "I have my refuge in the Gospel and in the flesh of Jesus," he wrote, "and in the Apostles as the presbytery of the Church."

Ignatius revered the sacred texts. "We love the prophets," he said, "because their preaching looked forward to the Gospel." But the Scriptures were not free-floating. They were ordered to "the flesh of Jesus," which was the sacrament of the Church, the sacrament of the New Testament.

Though he considers the written Scriptures to be sacred, they're subordinate to the proclamation they presuppose. Saint Ignatius wrote, "I hear some people saying,

'Unless I find it in the archives, I will not believe it in the Gospel.' I said to them, 'It is written...,' they answered me, 'That remains to be proved.' But as for me Jesus Christ *is* the archives. His cross, death, Resurrection, and faith through him, these are the archives." These unwritten "archives" (*archeia*) are in the custody of the Church, which for Ignatius is one and catholic.

Subsequent generations of the Fathers placed the same premium on tradition and succession. For Saint Irenaeus of Lyons, in the second century, the "tradition derived from the apostles...comes down to our time by means of the successions of the bishops." He singles out the Roman Church especially, and adds that "it is a matter of necessity that every Church should agree with this Church, on account of its pre-eminent authority." He then proceeds to list the bishops of Rome, in order, from Saint Peter down to Saint Eleutherius, then the current occupant of the papal throne. "In this order, and by this succession, the ecclesiastical tradition from the Apostles and the preaching of the truth have come down to us. And this is most abundant proof that there is one and the same vivifying faith, which has been preserved in the Church from the Apostles until now, and handed down in truth."

And so the faith continued to be "handed on," and we find a similar emphasis on succession and tradition in the authors in the centuries that followed. At the end of the third century, Eusebius of Caesarea began his massive work of Church history by sounding these familiar notes:

"It is my purpose to write an account of the successions of the holy Apostles, as well as of the times which have elapsed from the days of our Savior to our own...and those who in each generation have proclaimed the divine word either orally or in writing." As both a bishop and a historian, Eusebius recognized the value of succession and tradition.

From Clement through Eusebius, from Basil through Leo, the Fathers of the early Church knew—and not only knew, but took for granted—that every written *word of the New Testament* presupposed the enactment of the *liturgy of the New Testament* in the *Church of the New Testament*. The Gospels, the Epistles, and the Apocalypse were written to be read aloud in the Church's assembly, and some of these books even come with instructions for the lector (see Revelation 1:3 and 1 Thessalonians 5:27). The inspired documents mention the Church's ritual life, often in passing, as they refer to many other important matters. If they do not address the sacramental concerns of later centuries, it is because those questions never occurred to the Apostles, or to their successors who were faithful to the apostolic tradition...or to their successors, or to their successors.

CHAPTER 7

✠

The Old Testament in the New Testament

In the ancient world, worship provided the closest approximation to mass media. Since there was no large-scale production of books, the documents of the covenant were standardized not for editions to be printed, but for a word to be proclaimed. The proclamation was a solemn event, a ritual event. It was a liturgy. It was a time of remembrance, of calling to mind the terms of the covenant, and of recommitting to those terms. In the proclamation and the rites, the covenant was enacted anew—anew, yet in the traditional terms, the terms that had been handed on from "our fathers" (see, for example, John 6:31; Acts 13:17).

The covenant demanded verifiable continuity with the fathers (of Israel and, later, of the Church), and so it required standardization. This is the process that came later to be known as "canonization."

It seems that some such efforts were made long before the time of Christ. In the third century BC, Greek-speaking Jews in Egypt undertook a translation of the Hebrew Scriptures. In doing so, they implicitly acknowledged that the number of sacred books was limited and had been prescribed by tradition. That compilation, according to legend, was undertaken and completed by a team of seventy translators; and so it became known in Latin as the *versio septuaginta interpretum*, the "translation of the seventy interpreters," or Septuagint for short. It is the version often quoted by the Apostles, especially Saint Paul, and later by the Fathers of the Church. It was "Scripture." We may assume that when the books of the New Testament refer to "Scripture," as they often do, they are referring to an established, finite, commonly accepted, and easily verifiable collection of sacred writings.

To modern Christians, this may seem self-evident; but that is because we are heirs to half a millennium of mass media, centuries when standard editions could be produced and sent abroad in a matter of weeks or (now) even seconds.

In antiquity, Jews and Christians had no such technology, but they did standardize their holy books to a degree that historians find exceptional in the ancient world. We find such a "canon" implicit in the writings of the Christian Scriptures.

Jesus said repeatedly that "scripture must be fulfilled in me" (Luke 22:37), and "Scripture," for him, was something that "cannot be broken" (John 10:35). He used the term to describe the books of the Law (the Torah, the five books of Moses), the Prophets, and the Psalms. On the road to Emmaus, we see that "beginning with Moses and all the prophets, he interpreted to them in all the scriptures the things concerning himself" (Luke 24:27). The disciples who accompanied him recognize what has happened and remark, "Did not our hearts burn within us while he talked to us on the road, while he opened to us the scriptures?" (Luke 24:32). In the very next scene, we find Jesus at a similar meal with disciples, and once again "he opened their minds to understand the scriptures" (Luke 24:45).

"The Scriptures" in Jesus's generation are a story in search of an ending. They are a narrative of expectation. They hold out a promise made up of many promises, a certain event that would take place in the indeterminate future. The Scriptures of Israel, proclaimed in the liturgy of Temple and synagogue, trained the people to await a Messiah, an anointed king, a kingdom, an era of peace, a time of fidelity to God, the law, and true worship.

Thus Jesus could make his appeals and expect them to be understood, especially by scholars of the law. For he was, himself, the reason all the Scriptures had been given. He defined the Scriptures, quite simply, as "what is written about me," which now "has its fulfillment" (Luke 22:37). Because they are records of the promise, the Scriptures are permanently valid.

The proclamation of the New Testament always took the Old Testament as its starting point. We find this in the Acts of the Apostles when Philip encountered the Ethiopian eunuch as he was reading "Scripture," the book of Isaiah. "Then Philip opened his mouth, and beginning with this scripture he told him the good news of Jesus" (Acts 8:35).

For the Apostles, Jesus is the key to understanding the Old Testament. Apart from him the promises remain indeterminate and obscure. Saint Paul says of his Jewish kinsmen: "when they read the old covenant, that same veil remains unlifted, because only through Christ is it taken away" (2 Corinthians 3:14).

Through Christ the veil is taken away, but this takes place within the Church, and specifically in the Church's liturgy. Saint Peter is adamant about the necessity of the Church as the context for interpretation: "First of all you must understand this, that no prophecy of scripture is a matter of one's own interpretation" (2 Peter 1:20). In the next generation, Saint Polycarp would identify private interpretation as the mark of a "son of Satan."

The truth that the Church proclaimed began, very early, to take the form of brief creedal formulas. We find several of these in the earliest Christian documents, and they always sketch the saving work of Christ, confirmed by the Old Testament Scriptures, as read in the New Testament Church. For example, Saint Paul wrote to the Corinthians: "I delivered to you as of first importance what I also received, that Christ died for our sins *in accordance with the scriptures*, that he was buried, that he was raised on the third day in accordance with the *scriptures*" (1 Corinthians 15:3–4). The New Testament is simply what Paul has "received" through tradition, but it is confirmed by the Old Testament Scriptures it fulfills.

In the generation of the Apostles, there is no tension between Scripture and Church. Indeed, each is dependent upon the other, and each is inaccessible apart from the other. The New Testament's pastoral Epistles set Scripture as the authoritative source of the Church's discipline and order: "All scripture is inspired by God and profitable for teaching, for reproof, for correction, and for training in righteousness" (2 Timothy 3:16). "Scripture" is authoritative and inspired, but Paul and Timothy are charged by God with application of the Scriptures within the "church of the living God, the pillar and bulwark of the truth" (1 Timothy 3:15).

Already in the time of the Apostles, the very writings of the Apostles were revered in the same way. The Second Letter of Peter treats Saint Paul's letters as functionally equivalent to the books of the Old Testament: "So also our beloved brother Paul wrote to you according to the wisdom given him, speaking of this as he does in all his letters. There are some things in them hard to understand, which the ignorant and unstable twist to their own destruction, as they do the other scriptures" (2 Peter 3:15–16).

Thus, the Protestant Scripture scholar Richard Bauckham notes: "Apostolic writings must have ranked as authoritative writings, suitable for reading in Christian worship, long before there was any fixed NT canon."

By virtue of their office in the nascent Church, the Apostles definitively interpreted the word of the Old Testament in light of the dispensation of the New Testament. In this, they followed after their master who saw the Scriptures as books about himself—and not only his earthly ministry, but his Church and sacraments, too. To Jesus, the Old Testament manna, given to the Israelites in the desert, prefigured the "bread of life," the "bread come down from heaven," now given to the Church (John 6:49–50). To Saint Paul, the Israelites' passage through the Red Sea prefigured baptism (1 Corinthians 10:2); to Saint Peter, Noah's ark served the same purpose (1 Peter 3:20–21).

In the Old Testament Scriptures the entire New Testament was foreshadowed. In the New Testament dispensation, all the Old Testament Scriptures were fulfilled. As Saint Augustine put it: "The New Testament is concealed in the Old, and the Old Testament is revealed in the New."

The manner of fulfillment follows a discernible pattern. God has a characteristic way of dealing with humanity, and humanity has a fairly predictable way of responding to God. The pattern is, roughly, this: creation, fall, and redemption.

- God created Adam and Eve; they sinned; yet God let them live and even promised them a redeemer.
- God spared humanity and let it fill the earth. Yet humanity sinned again. So God punished the entire race, sparing the righteous Noah and his family.
- God called forth a people in Abraham. Yet they allowed themselves to become enslaved in Egypt. He redeemed them through the ministry of Moses.
- God gave his tribes a kingdom. Their kings neglected true worship and social justice, meriting invasion and exile. God anointed foreigners to bring a humbled people back to the land.

For God's chosen people, the wages of sin had precedents in Eden, in Egypt, in Babylon. The early Christians, like the prophets before them, discerned these patterns in the history of salvation. God's touches were like a recognizable watermark or trademark. The ancients called these foreshadowings "types"—in Greek, *typoi*—after the uniform mark left on an emperor's coin or on a wax seal. On a coin or a seal, a type symbolizes a ruler's authority. In the Scriptures, a type is itself a historical reality, but it is also representative of something greater. Moses prefigured Christ, though Moses was himself a man. The manna prefigured the Eucharist, though the manna was itself a miracle. In the New Testament, fulfillment was far greater than the sum of the Old Testament types. Fulfillment was the abiding presence of God himself: "And the Word became flesh and dwelt among us" (John 1:14). In the Church, the study and prayerful consideration of biblical types is called *typology*.

Human authors use words to symbolize realities. In salvation history, God uses temporal realities—even kings and kingdoms, laws and wars—to symbolize far greater realities, truths that are spiritual and eternal.

So the Scriptures, Old and New, were read aloud in the Mass of the early Christians. Saint Ignatius loved "the archives" because they forecast "the Gospel." Saint Justin Martyr said that at Mass in Rome in AD 150 "the memoirs of the apostles or the writings of the prophets are read, as long as time permits."

This was the Gospel the Apostles came to proclaim: God's promise in the Law and Prophets had been fulfilled in Jesus Christ. "In accordance with the Scriptures," Christ died; Christ is risen and exalted; Christ will come again. That was the content of Saint Paul's Gospel compressed in his First Letter to the Corinthians. We find similar creedal summaries in other New Testament Scriptures. They abound also in the works of the early Fathers, who referred to such a confession as a "canon of truth," *kanon tes aletheias*. In Greek, a *kanon* was a "ruler" or "measuring stick." So the Christians in the West came to call their short creeds the "rule of faith."

Old Testament promise and New Testament fulfillment: such was the "canon" in the first Christian century. History and necessity would assign another meaning to the term. And it all began when a wayward Christian refused to recognize the Old Testament in the New Testament.

✠

CHAPTER 8

The Canon of the New Testament

M arcion was a shipping magnate who lived on the Black Sea (in land that is now Turkey). Raised Christian, he got into moral trouble early in life and suffered the indignity of expulsion from the Church. That was, however, no impediment to business in a world that was predominantly pagan, and Marcion amassed a vast fortune in shipbuilding.

It was the mid-second century, around AD 140, and Christianity was slightly more than a century old. Yet the Church had spread rapidly, and its people already represented a small but significant subculture in many of the major cities of the Roman Empire, and not least in its capital, Rome, which had also become the center of gravity for the Church on earth.

Marcion decided to make his home there, amid the struggling Church, which had been intermittently persecuted since the days of Nero. Marcion gave extravagant gifts to the Church, succeeding in ingratiating himself with its leaders. In Rome, one could undertake study with fashionable teachers who claimed to be Christian, but who were definitely out of step with the bishops of the Catholic Church. They emphasized esoteric knowledge (in Greek, *gnosis*) over faith, and the spirit to the exclusion of the flesh.

Marcion may have been exposed to some of these teachers, and there are strains in his teaching that reflect developments of theirs, for example, his negative assessment of the material world and its creator. But Marcion's main work, as one early refutation put it, was to separate the law from the gospel; the God of justice and creation from the God of grace and redemption; the God of the Old Testament from the Father of Jesus Christ. This new God, revealed by Jesus, His eternal Son, offered release from the God of the Old Testament and his strict economy of law and justice. The grace of redemption meant that the God of the Old Testament, the Creator, and all his fleshly works, had simply been left behind, with the whole of the Old Testament, as irrelevant. The Old Testament, was not just "old," but "obsolete," with no scriptural status whatsoever for Marcion's Christian.

Marcion eventually let his religious opinions be known, to the horror of the Roman Church. He was summarily excommunicated and his donations returned—an act that certainly brought hardship upon the Church, which had recently begun its first large building projects.

Marcion was undeterred. He applied his entrepreneurial spirit to the promotion of his religion, investing shrewdly, and closely imitating his established competitor, the Catholic Church, in its rituals and structures. He poured his fortune into the dissemination of his ideas. Just ten years after Marcion's excommunication, Saint Justin Martyr observed that the Marcionite heresy had spread throughout the world.

Marcion may have been the first person to define a "canon" of New Testament texts. He published a much-trimmed version of Saint Luke's Gospel alongside ten of Saint Paul's Epistles, similarly scoured of any positive references to Israel, Judaism, or the Old Testament. He preferred Luke's Gospel because of its very favorable portrayal of gentiles. He called his collection the *Apostolikon*.

Many historians believe that it was Marcion's outrageous ambition that provoked the Church's first efforts to declare the books that had been received in the apostolic tradition, through the verifiable apostolic succession. The earliest list of canonical books we possess is from this period. It is known as the Muratorian Canon, and it probably dates from the generation after Marcion. Unfortunately, it survives only in fragmentary form. The unknown author lists four accepted Gospels, Acts, thirteen Pauline letters, two of John's letters, Jude, and the book of Revelation. Missing from the list are several books we consider canonical: Hebrews, First and Second Peter, and James.

Writing around the same time, Saint Irenaeus stated that there were four, and only four, authoritative Gospels, though he acknowledged a proliferation of spurious attempts at the genre, including a "Gospel" attributed to Judas Iscariot.

Saint Irenaeus held an almost unique authority to speak on these matters. He was a disciple of Saint Polycarp, who was himself a hearer of the Apostle John, so his experience of succession and tradition was very close to the ultimate historical source. He was a Christian from the Eastern Churches working in the West, so he had a lived experience of the Church's catholicity. He was, moreover, an ecclesial man, a priest and then a bishop in Gaul, but entrusted with special missions by the bishop of Rome—missions that affected the Church as a whole.

The heretics of Irenaeus's time were certainly industrious, and they succeeded in spreading disinformation and confusion. It's important for us to note, though, that none of the Gospels, Acts, Apocalypses, or "Epistles" put forward by these pretenders are from the apostolic age. They are all rather late creations; there is no evidence that any of them existed in the first century; and they do not reflect the Christian life or doctrine that we find in the historical record or the archeological record—or even the descriptions of the Church left by Christianity's persecutors. They are the fevered imaginings, rarely interesting, of Johnny-come-lately dissidents.

Their "gospels" spread and multiplied, however, like

poisonous mushrooms; and they required a response from the Church. This is the providential purpose of heresies. As Saint Augustine put it: "The effect of their activities is to assist the progress of the faithful…An argument aroused by an adversary turns out to be an opportunity for instruction."

::

It is interesting to note that none of the early authors apply the term "canon" to their lists of authoritative documents. Only at a relatively late date (the end of the fourth century), was the Greek word *kanon* applied to the list of biblical books. Writing in the late third and early fourth centuries, Eusebius employed a different term for the authoritative Scriptures, not *kanon*, but *diathēkē*. The writings that the Church acknowledged as authoritative, he said, had been "encovenanted"—in Greek, *endiathekai*. Thus, the sacred texts were, for the Church in the fourth century, the *covenantal documents*, the *testamental documents*. They were the only documents kept in God's presence in the sanctuary for the purpose of liturgical remembrance. They were the only texts that could be proclaimed in the New Testament liturgy.

The reality of the canon existed long before the term was applied to the contents of a book. Scholars will sometimes reconstruct the early Church's rules regarding Scripture by tracking which books the ancient authors cited with phrases denoting authority (such as "It is written…"). These compiled canons generally come close to the lists you'll find in the Bible as it's published today.

Authoritative lists became more common as the third century turned to the fourth, some produced by notables such as Saint Gregory of Nazianzus, Saint Cyril of Jerusalem, and Saint Epiphanius of Salamis.

The earliest complete record of the New Testament canon, exactly as we know it today, appears in AD 367 in the thirty-ninth Festal Letter of Saint Athanasius of Alexandria, the most revered theologian of his century. He had attended the Council of Nicaea (AD 325) as assistant to his bishop, Alexander; and it was that council that delegated the task of calculating the date of Easter to the Church of Alexandria. Athanasius's Festal Letters were the annual, authoritative announcement of Easter's date, determined according to traditional measures.

He took the occasion also to catechize the faithful in fundamental matters of faith; and so, in 367, he produced a list representing the New Testament canon. It matches perfectly with the table of contents you'll find in any Christian Bible produced in the twenty-first century.

Matthew
Mark
Luke
John
Acts

Romans

First Corinthians

Second Corinthians

Galatians

Ephesians

Philippians

Colossians

First Thessalonians

Second Thessalonians

First Timothy

Second Timothy

Titus

Philemon

Hebrews

James

First Peter

Second Peter

First John

Second John

Third John

Jude

Revelation

Saint Athanasius closes his list with these words: "These are the fountains of salvation, that he who thirsts may be satisfied with the living words they contain. In these alone the teaching of godliness is proclaimed. Let no one add to these; let nothing be taken away from them."

∷

Though not all the early lists agree in every detail, they do show forth a consensus of Christians throughout the world. What Saint Athanasius decreed in 367 soon found confirmation in Church synods (Rome in 382, Hippo Regius in 393, and Carthage in 419). Athanasius met no apparent opposition. The councils reached their decisions without evident rancor.

History shows us that the New Testament canon was the infallible decision of a Church that had the authority to make such a decision—and make it centuries after the last Apostle had died.

Some historians say that the definitive acts of canonization, so late in Christian history, are evidence of a growing "text-consciousness." Larry Hurtado proposes that it is "more correct to see an emergent *author-consciousness*." And that is certainly true. The apostolic origin of a text was indeed of paramount importance in the canonization process. Yet so was the apostolic origin of the authority of the bishops at Nicaea; and that authority—to recognize the very boundaries of divine Scripture—was not something newly emergent in 325. Before the bishops convened at Nicaea, apostolic succession had been a key concern in the historical works of Eusebius, the antiheretical theology of Irenaeus, the epistolary witness of Ignatius, and the pastoral letter of Clement.

Yet the urge to tinker with the New Testament documents, as Marcion had done, would show itself again in time. In the sixteenth century, Martin Luther expressed his opinion that Hebrews, James, Jude, and Revelation did not belong in the New Testament. At the beginning of the nineteenth century, Thomas Jefferson produced his own "Bible" *à la Marcion* that excised the Old Testament and reduced the New to a philosophy shorn of the supernatural. Even today, we will sometimes hear people refer to themselves as "New Testament Christians." Their God is presumably a kinder, gentler deity, tame in a way that the Old Testament Yahweh was not.

Behind many efforts to minimize the Old Testament, from Marcion to Jefferson and beyond, there lurks an unconscious anti-Semitism, an animus against Old Testament Law and culture. This is not to say that such people are bigots—the very idea would horrify them—but there is an implicit bias against Judaism in their dearly held notions. And that bias does not reflect biblical religion as we encounter it in primitive Christianity or in the classic formulas of the Fathers and the councils. As Pope Pius XI put it in the mid-twentieth century: "spiritually, we are all Semites." Christ himself preached from the Old Testament, recognized its authority, and spoke of it only in terms of reverence.

In the modern allergy to the Old Testament, we catch a whiff of Marcion's wish—that the ancient covenant would just go away and give way to a New Testament more to this or that individual's liking. All that the Old Testament *could* be for Marcion, or for the Gnostics who lived alongside him, was a relic of the Creator's tyranny.

For the Church, however, the Old Testament is essential to the New. The New Testament is unintelligible without it. Jesus died, rose, and was glorified, "in accordance with the Scriptures." That is the Christian rule of faith, now as ever. It is at the heart of our doctrine, our worship, and our life.

CHAPTER 9

✣

The New Testament and the Lectionary

W hen I was a Protestant pastor, there were books of the Bible I never proclaimed or preached in my churches' worship services: the New Testament Epistle of Saint Jude, for example, and the Old Testament book of Zephaniah. It's not that I considered those books to be unimportant. On the contrary, I revered them as the inspired word of God. It's just that there were other Scriptures that were more important, more interesting, and more relevant to the message I wanted to deliver. Jude's letter is very brief, full of historical curiosities that require explanatory background, and much of its material is repeated almost verbatim in the Second Letter of Saint Peter anyway! Zephaniah contains oracles related to our final judgment and the end times, but he remains a "minor prophet," eclipsed by the bigger books by bigger names: Isaiah, Jeremiah, Ezekiel, Daniel.

As pastor it was my job to choose each Sunday's

Scripture. Like most clergy in my denomination, I tended to choose just one reading, almost always from the New Testament. Even if I had remained in the pastorate for fifty years, it's unlikely that my congregations would ever have encountered Jude or Zephaniah in our worship services. I usually picked my weekly reading for the sake of the sermon I wanted to deliver. If I wanted to pack the maximum rhetorical power—to move the most hearts—I was going to choose most often from the words of Jesus himself, in the Gospels, or the rich theology of Saint Paul. I would return to certain texts repeatedly, while passing over wide swaths of Scripture that didn't serve my immediate purposes or pique my interest.

In other words, my congregation would receive the Bible as I represented it. They would encounter what I considered to be a "biblical worldview," but it was really based on a relatively small slice of the Scriptures. Nor was my church unusual in the evangelical world. I was following the methods I had learned in seminary, methods I refined by watching the pastors I most admired.

::

A Catholic priest could not get away with such an arrangement. Like his forebears in the Christian clergy, he is bound to use what tradition prescribes, what the Church has ordered for the day. He is required to follow the Church's lectionary.

The word "lectionary" comes from the Latin word *lectio*, which means "reading"—or, more precisely, a passage picked out (se-lected) for reading. Today, we ordinarily apply the word to a particular book used in the celebration of Mass. But the ancient lectionaries were simply lists of passages (called *lections* or *pericopes*) to be read in the liturgy on each given day. After consulting such a list, the Church's readers, called *lectors*, would then proclaim the prescribed passages directly out of the biblical books.

The Christian Church did not invent the lectionary. The Jewish Talmud tells us that the practice of standardizing readings for worship goes back to Moses himself. The synagogues of Jesus's day seem to have followed a cycle of readings to ensure that the entire five books of the Torah would be proclaimed in the course of a year. The Torah readings were accompanied by selections from the prophets and perhaps the Psalms as well. We see in Saint Luke's Gospel that when Jesus stood up to read in the synagogue "there was given to him the book of the prophet Isaiah" (Luke 4:17). It was not a passage Jesus chose. It was "given" according to the lectionary's requirement. Jesus's teaching, which followed, was based upon the reading he had been given.

Such reading was probably continuous: the selection *this* Sabbath picked up where the readings *last* Sabbath left off. For the major feasts—Passover, Pentecost, and Booths—the lectionary gave special readings that presented the day's historical background or that sounded the dominant themes of the feast.

It is possible that the first Christians, who were Jews, followed the lectionaries of the synagogue, supplemented gradually by the writings of the Apostles as they appeared. In Saint Paul's letters, Paul shows a keen awareness that his writings are inspired Scripture, because he urges that they be read aloud when the Church assembled (see, for example, Colossians 4:16 and 1 Thessalonians 5:27). Thus he instructed the churches to treat his letters as they treated the books of the Law and the Prophets: "Till I come, attend to the public reading of scripture, to preaching, to teaching" (1 Timothy 4:13).

As the works of Paul were used in this way—as well as the works of Peter, James, John, Jude, Matthew, Mark, and Luke—they became known collectively as the books of the New Testament. Why did they gain that title and not some other? Probably because of their association with the New Testament sacrifice. Saint Justin reports that the "memoirs of the Apostles" were read as a prelude to the Eucharistic offering in the middle of the second century. It would have seemed natural to extend the liturgy's title to the only books approved for proclamation in the liturgy. The canonical books were "the New Testament books" because they were proclaimed in the New Testament liturgy.

The Christian calendar, too, influenced the development of a Christian lectionary. The Church celebrated the vigil of Easter, the Christian Passover, with a series of specified readings. When we compare the seasonal sermons of the Church Fathers, who were separated by time as well as topography, we see evidence of a consensus regarding readings for other feasts and seasons as well: Christmas, Epiphany, the Baptism of Our Lord, Lent, Advent, and so on. The oldest surviving Christian lectionary comes from the fifth century and is attributed to Saint Jerome, the scholar who translated the Bible into Latin.

It was during the rise of Christianity that the "delivery system" for text gradually shifted from the scroll to the *codex*, bound stacks of folded sheets—paper "books" as we know them today—and Christians usually receive the credit for driving the technology. The codex had been around for centuries but had never caught on. Larry Hurtado notes that Christians found the codex extremely useful for liturgical applications. Codices could be bookmarked, and a lector could flip from section to section relatively easily. A codex could be laid upon an altar or lectern or held in hand during a public recitation. Hurtado observes also that the earliest biblical manuscripts include many aids for public reading: large lettering, spaces indicating pauses, generous space between lines of script, and division into obvious pericopes (the basis for later divisions by chapter and verse). "Christian manuscripts with these various scribal devices were prepared for ease of public reading in churches," Hurtado wrote. "That is, these small fragments probably give us further important artefactual evidence confirming second-century reports (e.g., Justin Martyr) of the liturgical practice of reading these New Testament writings."

::

The lectionary we currently use was published in 1969, but it draws upon millennia of refinement, the wisdom of the sages of ancient Israel and the saints of the Church. It assigns readings over the course of three years. Year A uses the Gospel According to Matthew, Year B uses Mark, and Year C uses Luke. Certain key passages from John—for example, Jesus's Bread of Life Discourse—are read on prescribed Sundays every year. John is also used frequently on feast days and throughout Lent, and to fill gaps left by the other Gospels, especially in Year B, since Mark's Gospel is very short.

So there are at least three hundred and sixty-five sets of liturgical readings every year. (Many days also have optional readings, for feasts of the saints.) There are four readings each Sunday and holy day: usually, a reading from the Old Testament, a Psalm, a reading from the New Testament books other than the Gospels (Acts, letters, Apocalypse), and, finally, a reading from the Gospel. By including books from both the Old and New Testaments, thematically coordinated, the Church ensures that we are always reading the New in light of the Old, and the Old in light of the New.

There is a world of difference between this system and what my congregations knew when I was a Protestant pastor. A priest who celebrates Mass daily is required to proclaim much of the Bible in the course of a three-year cycle. Catholics who attend daily Mass will hear much of the Bible read and preached again and again over the course of a lifetime. Those who attend every Sunday and holy day, which is the minimum the Church requires, will be sure to hear the most important passages repeated regularly.

The Catholic approach to Scripture is precisely opposite to the approach I used as a Protestant. In the Catholic Church today, as in the ancient Church, the readings are prescribed to suit the day, and the preaching should follow from the readings.

In fact, the Catholic schema proved so effective in communicating the Word of God that it was subsequently adapted by many Protestant bodies. It follows the earlier Catholic lectionary fairly closely, and it is used by congregations from a wide variety of traditions, from Anglican and Methodist to Presbyterian and Baptist. Historians may one day rank the 1969 lectionary as the most significant ecumenical advance of the twentieth century. Christians formerly divided from one another are now united on Sunday, at least in the readings they use in worship.

Since the lectionary itself is held in common by a growing number of Christians, Catholics and Protestants may find, more often than before, that they are "on the same page."

::

The lectionary's distribution of Scripture ensures the Church's dissemination of true doctrine. With the whole of the Bible proclaimed through the prism of the Church's feasts, the whole of Christian doctrine can reach the whole of Christendom. For Christian dogma is nothing other than the Church's authoritative interpretation of the Scripture.

In the ancient Church there was a saying: *Lex orandi, lex credendi.* Rough translation: The law of prayer is the law of belief. This has always been the way of biblical religion. People are formed by the way they worship. In offering the New Testament sacrifice, Christians receive the New Testament doctrine and it becomes part of us. It's like Mother Church feeding her children. The lectionary ensures that the children receive a balanced diet—not just consumption according to their own whims or their clergyman's idiosyncrasies.

One of the great modern rabbis, Samson Raphael Hirsch, once said that the catechism of the Jew is the calendar. Though we Christians do have useful catechisms, the statement is doubly true for us as well.

Why is the calendar a catechism? Because the feasts require the proclamation of God's Law, within a context that is both historical (and thus empirical) and worshipful (and thus spiritual). In worship the Word is incarnate, and that flesh feeds our own, becomes our own.

Archbishop José Gomez, of Los Angeles, California, speaks poetically about this process.

> [T]here is a purpose and a spiritual power in the Church's liturgical cycle of readings, especially in the Gospels. During the course of the Church's liturgical year, we are presented day by day with the life of Christ—his Incarnation, birth, and "hidden life"; his public teaching and ministry; his passion and death; his Resurrection, ascension and sending of the Holy Spirit. Through this cycle of readings, Blessed [Columba] Marmion said, "the Church leads us by the hand in Jesus' footsteps. We have only to listen, only to open the eyes of faith: we are following Jesus."
>
> Following Jesus, contemplating these mysteries, our love for him grows and we gradually come to a deeper understanding of the heart and the mind of Christ. Through our daily encounter we are being refashioned in the *imago Christi*, through the power of God's Word working in us.

That's the glorious dispensation of the New Testament. That's Good News.

✠

CHAPTER 10

Trusting the Testaments:

The Truth and Humility of the Word

The biblical testaments are not reducible to words. We have seen that again and again. They derive their significance, above all, from their proximity to the mighty deeds of God, whether in history or in the sacraments.

The biblical testaments are not reducible to words. They are, however, identifiable with the Word. In the New Testament we see that there is a close relationship between the *pages of Scripture* and the *person of Jesus*. We call them both by the same word, which in Greek is *Logos* and in English, *Word*. Scripture is the Word inspired; Jesus is the Word Incarnate (see John 1:1; Revelation 19:13). In the Bible, the divine Word is expressed in human language; in Jesus, the divine Word takes flesh in human nature. The two mysteries illuminate each other.

It is Jesus who sets the standard for what the Church believes and teaches about the Bible. It's Christ's vision of the Bible that determines how Christians view the Bible. He is "the pioneer and perfecter of our faith" (Hebrews 12:2). By his teaching and example, the *Word made flesh* shows his followers how to understand the *Word made Scripture*.

In the Gospels, Jesus appeals often to the sacred texts of the Old Testament. He does so in his preaching, in his private temptations, and in dialogue with opponents. He always acts and thinks in accord with biblical revelation. He quotes the texts of the Old Testament at least forty times throughout the four Gospels. But this figure fails to do justice to his devotion, since countless other times he alludes to the biblical writings in more subtle and sophisticated ways—adopting their vocabulary, using their images, expounding their themes. It is no exaggeration to say that the mind of Jesus was saturated with the teachings and concerns of the Scriptures.

His most basic conviction was that Scripture had its origin in God. For Jesus, the words of the Bible are the words of his Father; and so its written assertions are nothing less than divine assertions preserved in readable form. Consider Matthew 19:4–5, where Jesus regards "what Scripture says" and "what God says" as one and the same thing. In discussing the divine plan for married life, he tells the Pharisees that "he who made" man and woman in the beginning is also the One who said, "Therefore a man leaves his father and his mother and cleaves to his wife, and they become one flesh" (Genesis 2:24). Thus, according to Jesus, the voice of the world's Creator is the same voice that speaks through the human words of the book of Genesis.

We see the same disposition at work in Mark 12:36, where Jesus refers to David being "inspired by the Holy Spirit" when he composed the words of Psalm 110. Jesus envisions David, the human psalmist, cooperating in a supernatural movement of the Spirit, uttering words that ultimately point to Jesus's own status as the Christ, the Messiah. Here, because the Spirit oversaw the writing of the Scriptures, the words have a *divine* cause; at the same time, a *human* author scrawled his thoughts on papyrus, and that is just as naturally a part of the picture. Thus, Jesus gives credit for the sacred writings to God, but he also affirms the conscious involvement of human authors. He also speaks of other portions of the Bible being written by other human beings: Moses (John 5:46–47), Isaiah (Mark 7:6), and Daniel (Matthew 24:15).

If Scripture's origin is divine, its authority must be supreme. If the Bible represents the discourse of God, it must express the will of God. Jesus reveals this most memorably during his showdown with the devil in the wilderness. In Saint Matthew's account of the temptations of Jesus, the Messiah repels the devil with three quotations from the Old Testament Scriptures. In all three, he introduces the citation with the preface "it is written," a formula used in Judaism and throughout the New Testament to summarize the belief that Scripture is the ultimate foundation for religious faith and life (Matthew 4:4, 7, 10). Jesus confirms this by his first quotation against the devil in Matthew 4:4: "Man shall not live by bread alone, but by every word that proceeds from the mouth of God" (Deuteronomy 8:3).

Since Scripture communicates words that come from God, it lays down inviolable standards that must never be ignored or transgressed. Jesus states in John 10:35 that "scripture cannot be broken."

The question will then arise: If Scripture comes from God, and if its teachings have divine authority, does it follow that Scripture is divinely truthful? Jesus's answer, which emerges from the Gospels, is an emphatic yes. Consider his "high priestly prayer" in John 17:1–26. Petitioning the Father on behalf of his disciples, he states: "thy word is truth" (John 17:17). Such an assertion would be deprived of meaning if in fact the written Word of God were tainted with misinformation.

Christ firmly believed that the Old Testament "must" be brought to fulfillment in him, especially in the events of his suffering, death, and Resurrection; for the Scriptures had determined in advance that he should be handed over to enemies (Matthew 26:54), "reckoned with transgressors" (Luke 22:37), lifted up on the Cross (John 3:14), and brought through suffering into glory (Luke 24:25–26). It is hard to imagine such a weight of divine necessity on the mind of Jesus unless he was convinced of the absolute truth of the sacred texts. Jesus maintained that the entire Old Testament bears witness to his mission.

All of this takes on greater significance when we consider that Jesus's whole mission was "to bear witness to the truth" (John 18:37) and to enable his disciples to "know the truth" by sticking to his word (John 8:31–32). He claims for himself a personal veracity that, for anyone else, would be outrageous and just plain crazy. Not even the prophets of Israel, who spoke by the Spirit of God, could make such all-encompassing claims for their teaching.

The authority and reliability of God's Word in Scripture stands or falls with the authority and reliability of God's Word Incarnate. The two are inseparably united at the deepest level.

::

Jesus's perspective on Scripture was immediately taken up as the perspective of the early Church. There is no clearer statement than Paul's affirmation in 2 Timothy 3:16–17: "All scripture is inspired by God and profitable for teaching, for reproof, for correction, and for training in righteousness, that the man of God may be complete, equipped for every good work." The crucial expression of the passage is "inspired by God," which in Greek is the compound adjective *theopneustos*, meaning "breathed by God." As God breathes life into his human creation (see Genesis 2:7), so he "breathes forth" the Scriptures.

Human words are merely a breath, a bit of air accompanied by a momentary sound. But the breath of the Lord is an instrument of his infinite power. It brought all of creation into being (Psalm 33:6) and performed such mighty feats of deliverance as blasting a path of escape through the Red Sea (2 Samuel 22:16). To say that Scripture is "God-breathed" is to speak of its divine origin as well as its divine power. "Inspired" Scripture is a word that never fails to accomplish God's purpose (see Isaiah 55:11).

So much for the divine source of the Scriptures, but what about the historical process by which they're produced? Saint Peter speaks of this when he declares: "First of all you must understand this, that no prophecy of scripture is a matter of one's own interpretation, because no prophecy ever came by the impulse of man, but men moved by the Holy Spirit spoke from God" (2 Peter 1:20–21). Peter is anxious to deny that biblical prophecy is a strictly natural phenomenon, as though the prophets of Israel communicated only what they imagined the future would bring. Peter counters such mistaken notions with the conviction that every prophecy of Scripture comes about by a supernatural operation of the Spirit. Peter emphasizes the prophet's role of speaking a divine message in oral form (v. 21), but he also has in view the permanent expression of the oracles in the written texts of the Bible (v. 20).

Peter describes the divine influence upon the prophets in terms of men being "moved" by the Spirit. The

Spirit is more than a helper. The Spirit determines what the prophet utters, much as a strong wind determines the course and nautical speed of a ship driven out to sea (as in Acts 27:15, 17). By the same token, the saying does not imply that the prophets were merely passive instruments manipulated by an irresistible force. Peter has in mind the writing prophets of the Bible, and these must not be confused with ecstatic prophets whose faculties were seized by the Spirit and put to use in an altered state of consciousness. Rather, the prophets whose writings became part of the Bible were free and active participants in an activity that was both human and divine.

Furthermore, because the prophecies of Scripture were given "by" the divine Spirit, and because the prophets articulated words that originated "from" God as their Source, Peter concludes that readers have every reason to place full confidence in their message. This is why he insists that the prophetic word is so "sure" (2 Peter 1:19). Guaranteed by God, prophetic oracles can always be trusted to reach their fulfillment, even if they appear to be delayed and are forced to suffer the ridicule of scoffers and heretics (topics of discussion in 2 Peter 2–3).

::

God speaks directly to his people through the biblical texts. Regardless of when the books of Scripture may have been written, the speech of God travels the ages to address the present situation of the faithful. An example of this appears in Hebrews 3:7, where the Holy Spirit is said to speak the words of Psalm 95:7–8 to believers in the first century. The passage is put forward as immediately relevant to the original recipients of the Letter to the Hebrews, not because the ancient psalmist had this community in mind when he wrote, but because the Spirit "says" (present tense) what the Psalm says in the here and now. The voice of the human author had long since fallen silent, and yet the voice of God, proceeding from eternity, is contemporary with every generation that encounters his Word.

What we find in the New Testament is confirmed clearly and unambiguously by the earliest Fathers of the Church. Already in the first century, Saint Clement of Rome tells the Corinthians that the Holy Scriptures are "true" and that "nothing unrighteous or counterfeit is written in them." In the middle of the second century, Saint Justin Martyr counters accusations against the internal consistency of the Bible with the emphatic declaration: "I am positive that no passage [of Scripture] contradicts another." And before the close of the second century Saint Irenaeus of Lyons contends that "the Scriptures are indeed perfect, since they were spoken by the Word of God and his Spirit."

There are no statements to the contrary, either in the New Testament or in the earliest mainstream traditions. So we are left to conclude that historically the Christian perspective on the Bible is unbroken. From Jesus to the apostolic Church to the pastors and theologians of the second century there is full unanimity of conviction on Scripture's divine origin, divine authority, and divine truthfulness. This doctrine echoes down to modern times, from the First Vatican Council to the Second Vatican Council, and in many statements by the popes.

⁘

It is no surprise, though, that some people find it difficult to embrace the "high view" of Scripture advocated by Jesus and the Church. These claims on faith are unverifiable from a scientific standpoint, and they seem improbable from a rational standpoint. To put it bluntly, the written Word of God strikes some people as too human to be divine. Intellectuals throughout history have thus faced the scandal of the Bible and chosen to reject it. In this way too the inspired Word treads the path of the incarnate Word and reflects its mystery.

Scripture will always be a reflection of the Word made flesh. The perfect sinlessness of Jesus is comparable to the perfect truthfulness of the Bible. But what about the fact that Jesus was despised as an uneducated and ordinary man claiming to wield divine authority? Even in this respect the Scriptures bear the image of the crucified Messiah. For the texts of the Bible, by presenting their mighty claims in such modest garb, are offensive to human pride and draw the contempt of the snobs and self-regarding sophists of every age.

Yet they draw the humble seeker. In the second century, Tatian, a disciple of Saint Justin Martyr, confessed: "I was led to put faith in the Scriptures by the unpretentious cast of the language, the candid character of the writers, and yet the foreknowledge displayed of human events."

As Saint Paul put it, "we have this treasure in earthen vessels" (2 Corinthians 4:7). The third-century biblical scholar Origen explained: "By 'earthen vessels' we understand the humble diction of the Scriptures, which the Greeks are so ready to despise, but in which the excellence of God's power appears so clearly."

⠶

The Bible is not just authentically human, but sometimes scandalously human. The less-than-appealing features of the Word often present stumbling blocks to a belief in the Bible's divine perfection. Scripture has a tendency to speak in one place of God having human feelings such as wrath (see Romans 2:5), and then elsewhere to say that he is a pure spirit (see Isaiah 31:3; John 4:24). Many have scorned these as the crude and confused conceptions of an uncultivated people. One could also point to Scripture's unpolished diction, a feature that has always put off educated minds with more refined literary tastes. And its penchant for hyperbole and poetic license fails to captivate those who think that the Bible should speak only with scientific exactitude. Still more scandal arises from the alleged discrepancies that make the Bible appear inconsistent with itself, with the documents of ancient history, and with the findings of modern science.

The collective impression of these "blemishes" causes proud minds to recoil and refuse consent. It is a reminder that unbelief will always remain an option and even the default position of many who find no way to account for Scripture's apparent lack of sophistication.

The question is whether these humble aspects of the Word should stand as barriers to our acceptance of its supernatural authority and reliability.

They should not. In fact, I would say that the way the Bible communicates is perfectly harmonious with the mystery of Christ himself. The same rationale that underlies the Incarnation of the Eternal Word also informs the inspiration of the scriptural Word. Neither is intelligible except as an instance of divine condescension—God stooping down, like a father, to address his children. He bends down to make contact with people in ways that are fitted to their capacity to receive him. God lowers himself in view of our weakness with the aim of lifting us up by his strength.

Thus, divine accommodation is not primarily a matter of the human dimension of revelation limiting the divine but of the divine making known and being rendered comprehensible through the human. The Word Incarnate accomplished this by the assumption of a human nature; the Word inspired achieves this by making use of simple human language. The challenge is to keep the full reality in view as we interpret the Bible. Even when God packages his perfection and power in lowly tangible forms, we must not allow their sensible exterior to blindfold us to their supernatural interior.

The supreme example of divine condescension is the Son, who "emptied himself" to become a man (Philippians 2:7). The Eternal Word accepted the limitations and weaknesses of the human condition. The New Testament testifies that Jesus experienced such things as fatigue (John 4:6), hunger (Matthew 4:2), astonishment (Mark 6:6), grief (John 11:35), and extreme distress (Luke 22:44). Ultimately, he "humbled himself" to the point of accepting death, "even death on a cross" (Philippians 2:8). Yet virtually none of these empirical observations, which confirm the full humanity of Jesus, forces us to conclude that Christ divested himself of his divinity or surrendered his inherent flawlessness and sinlessness. The weaknesses apparent on the surface of Jesus's historical life do not cancel or diminish his unseen perfection. At no point did he cease to be "the truth" (John 14:6), the sinless Word of the Father (Hebrews 4:15; 1 Peter 2:22).

The same is true of the written Word of God. Despite its concrete expression in human language—even plain and sometimes imperfect language—it does not cease to be the divine speech of God. The Word Incarnate was intensely human, yet he never sinned. So too the Word inspired is intensely human, yet it never errs. Once again it is Jesus who is the key to understanding the mystery of Scripture as simultaneously human and divine, as imperfect in appearance but perfect in reality. In this respect, the Church's belief in biblical inspiration and biblical inerrancy is simply an extension of her faith in the Incarnation.

And yet inerrancy by itself does not prove a work's divine inspiration. Other books may also be free from error. A well-edited math textbook in its third edition may be scrubbed of all typos and flawless in its equations, but no one will say it is divinely inspired.

Biblical inspiration consists of the Spirit conveying the Word of God through fallible human instruments. But the Spirit continues to bear the Word into the world through the liturgy—the New Testament sacrifice of the Holy Mass. This is accomplished through proclamation of the document as well as administration of the sacrament. In the Eucharistic assembly, the biblical Word is read aloud, speaking anew to God's people yet inviting them to respond with the same "obedience of faith" (Romans 1:5; 16:26) that the first Christians gave. Likewise, by the simultaneous action of the Spirit and human speech the Word is made present and *made food*. This makes every occasion of sacramental worship a new intervention of God in history, a new event of salvation, and a new creation as well (see 2 Corinthians 5:17).

Here the power of God working through human weakness is unmistakable. God continues to use the frailest of natural means to accomplish his supernatural purposes. Empowered by grace, the priest is made to act in the person of Christ, speaking his words, repeating his movements, and setting before us the paschal sacrifice that redeemed the world. And the humble elements of bread and wine that stand helpless before the transubstantiating Word—these are the lowly signs that will be made the Lord's greatest gift. It is difficult to imagine a more self-abnegating form by which the divine Word should signal his presence among us than the form he uses in the New Testament sacrifice.

::

Why should God express himself and his will in the humble letter of the Bible? My own conviction is that it invites reason to embrace the knowledge of faith, and that it confronts pride with a summons to intellectual humility.

The humility of the Word first of all represents a challenge to the supremacy of reason in our understanding of reality. We are prone to forget that reason has limitations. Not only is the intellectual faculty incapable of demonstrating the mysteries of faith, but it is strictly incapable of discerning the presence and actions of God in history. This is a serious handicap when it comes to interpreting the Bible. I'm not saying that we should retreat into pious credulity in our study of Scripture, but rather that we should avoid the irrationality of pure rationalism. Reason functions properly when we accept its limitations and acknowledge that there are questions it cannot answer.

The humble expression of the Word invites us to be healed of intellectual arrogance. The fact is that even when faith and reason are working in tandem, the latter is tempted to impose unreasonable restrictions on the former. In the realm of biblical studies, this takes the form of skepticism, what scholars sometimes call "a hermeneutic of suspicion." This approach means not only that the Bible's sincerity and truthfulness must be proven before the Word can be accepted, but also that the interpreter stands in a position of judgment over the Word, measuring its claims according to his or her own standards.

This turns things upside down. The folly of divine condescension urges that we lay aside our educated conceit in approaching the biblical Word. It calls for an intellectual humility in which the mind adjusts itself to the mode of God's revelation—in a sense, lowering itself to the same level! An intellect that is humble and receptive to the Word in modest dress is one that tunes itself to the higher wisdom of God and receives the insight that is withheld from "the wise and understanding" (Matthew 11:25). It recognizes the truth that God's "power is made perfect in weakness" (see 2 Corinthians 12:9).

We have only to turn to the Gospels to see what this means in practice. Jesus embodies the response of personal humility that the form of the written Word requires. Hearing the Scriptures as the voice of the Father, he allowed himself to be formed by its message in all aspects of his human life. He lovingly fulfilled his commitments as a devout Jew. He followed the rhythms of life and the dictates of the Hebrew Scriptures as proclaimed in the weekly synagogue liturgies and the yearly Temple festivals. His comprehensive familiarity with the biblical writings bears witness to his full participation in the religious observances of his people. Even at the point of agony and death, the memorized words of the Psalter fall from his parched lips (Mark 15:34 = Psalm 22:1; Luke 23:46 = Psalm 31:5). Everywhere his attitude toward the Bible is one of docility and total adherence to its authority and truth.

This is remarkable considering that Christ is the Word of God begotten from eternity (John 1:1). He is the full disclosure of God in the world, the living sacrament of the kingdom of God, which he proclaims. Jesus's submission to the Bible can only be called an act of extreme humility. It is a profound gesture of self-abasement for the Word made flesh to surrender himself in reverent obedience to the Word made Scripture. And yet it is entirely in keeping with his character. Jesus is, after all, the Eternal Word who entered time in a manger, suffered on a cross, and gave himself as common bread.

For those of us who read the Bible, responding to the humility of the biblical Word means imitating the incarnate Word in all of this. His example suggests it, and his very words demand it: "Take my yoke upon you, and learn from me; for I am gentle and lowly in heart" (Matthew 11:29).

✛

CHAPTER II

The New Testament and Christian Doctrine

Heresies have been with the Church since the beginning. Some of them, like Marcion's, were outright rejections of scriptural teaching, demanding the excision of entire portions of the Bible. But most of the heresies were not. They were not about rejection of Scripture, but rather about deep differences over its interpretation. Such heretics were arguing not against the Bible, but against the Church's interpretation of the Bible.

Consider the movement that saw the greatest growth in antiquity, the heresy of Arianism. It started with a priest in the city of Alexandria, in Egypt. Renowned as a scholar, preacher, and ascetic, Arius refused to worship Jesus as God. His justification, he said, was in the Old Testament book of Proverbs, where personified Wisdom says: "The Lord created me at the beginning of his work, the first of his acts of old" (Proverbs 8:22). For Arius, this verse clearly referred to Christ, and spoke of him as a creature—neither coeternal nor coequal with the Father. He found confirmation, he said, in the words of Jesus himself: "the Father is greater than I" (John 14:28), as well as in the words of Saint Paul, who calls Christ the "first-born of all creation" (Colossians 1:15).

Arius forced a crisis when he loudly interrupted a homily preached by his bishop, Alexander. The bishop attempted a reconciliation, but failed to persuade Arius, who was then excommunicated along with his followers in 318 or 319. None of this deterred Arius. He was a master preacher who claimed to present the plain sense of Scripture. In fact, he scrupulously avoided theological terms that fell outside the biblical vocabulary, calling Bible things by Bible names. He was adept at sloganeering. He taught his followers short phrases like "There was once when he was not," to refer to Jesus's supposed creation in time. Some followers even set his slogans to catchy music, to spread the word more effectively.

In worldly terms, Arius had a lot going for him: scholarly credentials, excellent preaching skills, good music, and memorable slogans. He persuaded many people, including bishops and emperors, to come over to his side. So swift and sweeping was his success that Saint Jerome complained: "The world awoke to find itself Arian."

The first ecumenical council, the Council of Nicaea in 325, was called to settle the Arian controversy. There the council fathers ruled against Arius, stating that the Son is *homoousios* with the Father—that is, he is of the same substance with the Father. The Arian party objected that the term *homoousios* was nowhere to be found in the Bible, and thus was an inappropriate application of pagan philosophical terms to Christian theology.

Some Christians concluded (rightly) that the controversy couldn't be settled by simple recourse to scriptural texts. Arius had piled up his proof texts, and his opponents had piled up theirs. So a party within the Church proposed a compromise, a different word that both opponents might accept. It was *homoiousios*, "of like substance." With the addition of just a single letter, the compromisers argued, the creed could accommodate Arius, who believed the Father had conferred a sort of divinity upon Jesus, while still accommodating the Nicene party, whose belief would be subsumed under the altered phrase.

Saint Athanasius refused, as did the Church, because the compromise would have denied Jesus the worship he was due within the Church—worship he had received since the time of the Apostles. While Arius had returned repeatedly to the New Testament document, Athanasius had read the New Testament document in light of the New Testament sacrament—in communion with the Church. In the Eucharistic liturgies, Jesus was clearly professed, proclaimed, worshipped, and received as God, coeternal and coequal with the Father. For Athanasius—and for the Church—it was the law of prayer that proved the law of faith, when "Scripture alone" could not do it.

What settled the Arian controversy was not a book, but rather the Church as the Apostles had established it: with succession, tradition, a liturgy, sacraments, and saints.

⠃

The Arian crisis was not the last time the Church had to speak dogmatically to settle a disputed point of biblical interpretation. Yet such controversies press the Church on to deeper study, deeper contemplation, and richer development of the apostolic tradition that was given once for all.

Because so many of the crises are about interpretation, the Church's dogma is never far from the pages of Scripture. As Cardinal Joseph Ratzinger (later Pope Benedict XVI) put it: "Catholic dogma...derives all its content from Scripture." Elsewhere he states that "Dogma is by definition nothing other than an interpretation of Scripture." Dogma, then, is the Church's infallible interpretation of the sacred text.

There is no contradiction, no opposition, between the Jesus of history and the Christ of Catholic dogma. Indeed, the Jesus of history is unknowable except as the Christ of dogma, whom the Council of Nicaea confirmed to be the anointed Son of the Father.

The Church's body of dogmatic and doctrinal teaching forms a rich deposit of reflection on the sacred Word. The earliest dogmatic statements, the creeds, consisted of articles of faith composed from the words of Scripture. Later, faced with complex heresies, the Church's popes and bishops developed an "auxiliary" theological vocabulary of extra-biblical terms and concepts to assist them in safeguarding the true reading of the Gospels from error and heresy—words like *homousios* (one in being), *Trinitas* (Trinity), and *Theotokos* (God-bearer or Mother of God), and formulations like "original sin," "transubstantiation," and "immaculate conception." Of such terms Saint Athanasius said: "Even if the expressions are not in so many words in the Scriptures, yet they contain *the sense of the Scriptures*; and, expressing it, they convey it to those who have their hearing unimpaired for religious doctrine."

But even these new doctrinal and dogmatic terms, though not themselves found in the Scripture, are implicit in the inspired texts and point back to those texts. And the language of Scripture remains "referential" for the Church—that is, it is privileged and fundamental, not only for teaching the faith and evangelization, but for prayer and spiritual formation, too.

What does this mean for our understanding of Scripture? First, that in reading and interpreting any passage of Scripture we can never detach ourselves from the way that Scripture is read and interpreted in the official magisterial documents of the Church. This is not just a negative test, or an out-of-bounds line. It is true that the Church has been given the Holy Spirit to help it guard and interpret the Word, so all our judgments about a given passage will need to conform to how the Spirit has guided the Church to read this passage.

This is not a limitation on our creativity as interpreters. In fact, it empowers us, gives us new powers of insight into the sacred texts. What the Church calls the "analogy of faith"—the coherence and connections that intertwine all of the Church's doctrines and dogmas—is also positive and problem-solving. It shows the explanatory power of dogma. There are powerful interpretive clues found implicitly in Catholic dogmas that give us privileged insights into the meaning of texts. Dogmas do not just tell us when our reading has gone afoul. Dogmas will illuminate some of the dark corners in difficult texts in the Old and New Testaments.

✠

CHAPTER 12

The Mysterious Plan in the New Testament

W hen the later Fathers talked about the two testaments, they delighted in emphasizing the unity of the two as one book. Against the Marcionites and Gnostics who rejected the Old Testament, Tertullian defended the Catholic Church that "unites in one volume the law and the prophets with the writings of evangelists and apostles, from which she drinks in her faith."

What unites both testaments, for the Fathers as for the Apostles, was the plan of God, what Saint Paul called "the plan of the mystery" (Ephesians 3:9; 1:10), what we might call "the big picture." For the first Christians, God's plan was a most ancient mystery whose story line had been partially disclosed "in many and various ways" as "God spoke of old…by the prophets" (Hebrews 1:1), but was fully revealed only in the person and saving work of Jesus Christ. The great twentieth-century Dominican Yves Congar said that for the early Church "the content and meaning of Scripture was God's covenant plan, finally realized in Jesus Christ…and in the Church."

The Greek word for "plan" used by Saint Paul—and, later, the Fathers—was *oikonomia*, from which we get the English word "economy." By economy, they meant not the movement of capital and the division of labor, but rather (to take its most literal rendering) "the law of the family." *Oikonomia* is how a father administers his household, the disposition of its property, the arrangement of family members, and the inheritance. The divine economy, then, is God's fatherly plan for his people in history and in eternity. We find this sense throughout Saint Paul's letters and in the writings of the earliest of the Fathers. Saint Ignatius of Antioch wrote: "For our God, Jesus Christ, was, according to the economy of God, conceived in the womb by Mary, of the seed of David, but by the Holy Spirit."

The economy is what we discover when we, like our most ancient ancestors in the faith, read the Old Testament in light of the New Testament and the New in light of the Old. The mystery hidden for all ages has been revealed in Christ.

As it unfolds in the pages of sacred Scripture, the divine economy proceeds in a series of *covenants* that God makes with his people. Saint Irenaeus said that "the divine program and economy for the salvation of humanity" is revealed when we study how God made "several covenants with humanity, not just one, along with the special character of each covenant."

In our culture and time we are almost tone-deaf to the biblical meaning of covenant. For most of us, "covenant" means a sort of contract. But contracts are entered into by two parties who agree to exchange goods or services according to specific terms and conditions. A covenant is not a deal to exchange things, but a promise of one's self, an oath that forges kinship bonds, family ties. Covenants make of two parties one family, flesh and blood.

The classic covenant formula in Scripture is God's promise: "I will be your God and you will be my people." God's promise is always matched by an oath sworn by the people, an act of faith, a pledge to keep the covenant (Leviticus 26:12; see also Exodus 6:7; 2 Corinthians 6:16–18). With each succeeding covenant in Scripture—with Adam and Eve on the seventh day of creation and with Noah after the flood, with Abraham, Moses, and David, and finally with the New Covenant written in the blood of Jesus—God reveals more fully his desire to fashion all humanity into his family. With each succeeding covenant, he reveals more fully his intention to raise human beings up to be his divine sons and daughters, partakers of his blessedness, his divine nature (2 Peter 1:4).

Christ's New Covenant fulfills all "the covenants of promise," and in his Catholic or universal Church he establishes a new "household of God" (Ephesians 2:12, 19), a worldwide kingdom, a divine family, "a chosen race, a royal priesthood, a holy nation, God's own people" (1 Peter 2:9; see also "kingdom of priests" in Revelation 1:6 and 5:10). We pledge ourselves to this New Covenant. We enter Christ's family as adopted sons and daughters, through an act of faith in the sacramental liturgy of his Church. Indeed, as we noted earlier, the word "sacrament" comes from the Latin *sacramentum,* which means "oath."

By the oath we swear in the sacrament of baptism, we receive the gift of the Holy Spirit (which enables us to keep Christ's New Covenant), his New Testament, and to call God our Father (Galatians 4:6–7; Romans 8:15). By the oath we swear in the Eucharist, we renew our covenant bond, become ever more "the flesh and blood" of God (1 Corinthians 10:16; 11:26). This New Covenant is not the end of salvation history, but rather the beginning of its last days. The New Covenant will be fulfilled in the glorious return of Christ, a day the Bible's last book describes in covenantal language—"Behold, the dwelling of God is with men. He will dwell with them, and they shall be his people, and God himself will be with them" (Revelation 21:3).

The goal of the divine economy, then, is revealed in the covenants by which God punctuates salvation history, and it is nothing less than full communion between God and humanity, "the marriage supper of the Lamb" (Revelation 19:9). In such communion, the human family is "divinized," made to dwell with God, made full participants in the divine life of the Trinity.

::

Scripture, then, read as the Word of God in the living tradition of the Church—read in the Spirit in which it was written by the inspired authors—reveals God's economy, his covenantal plan for his children. Covenant, then, becomes the master key for understanding God's ways of revealing himself to his children.

And when we study the covenants in Scriptures, we discover a particular pattern by which God communicates to his children in history. We discover what Paul and the Fathers called the divine "pedagogy." A pedagogy is a method of teaching. The Fathers described God's pedagogy as that of a loving parent, instructing his people as a parent instructs a child, gradually building the child's confidence and knowledge until he or she grows into maturity.

In the third century, the Egyptian scholar Origen said that God revealed himself by means of "baby talk"— "talking a little language to his children, like a father caring for his own children and adopting their ways." Saint Gregory of Nazianzen said: "In the various manifestations of God to man he both adapts himself to man and speaks in human language...so that through feelings corresponding to our own infantile life, we might be led as by the hand and lay hold of the Divine nature by means of words which his foresight has given."

The Scriptures, then, when read in the way they were intended to be read, can be seen as one long story of the

Father instructing his children, teaching them and testing them, preparing them for divine life, for life in the Spirit as his sons and daughters. God proceeds according to a discernible method of pedagogy. This is how Saint Augustine put it:

> The education of the human race, represented by the people of God, has advanced, like that of an individual, through certain epochs, or, as it were, ages, so that it might gradually rise from earthly to heavenly things, and from the visible to the invisible. This object was kept so clearly in view, that, even in the period when temporal rewards were promised, the one God was presented as the object of worship, that men might not acknowledge any other than the true Creator and Lord of the spirit, even in connection with the earthly blessings of this transitory life... It was best, therefore, that the soul of man, which was still weakly desiring earthly things, should be accustomed to seek from God alone even these petty temporal boons, and the earthly necessities of this transitory life, which are contemptible in comparison with eternal blessings, in order that the desire even of these things might not draw it aside from the worship of Him, to whom we come by despising and forsaking such things.

In all of this we see a pattern of accommodation—a twofold movement of divine condescension and elevation, of descent and ascent. We see God stooping down to the level of his beloved yet lowly children in order to raise them up to his own level, to share in the divine nature. In his accommodation, the Father leads his children to the spiritual by means of the material, to the eternal by way of the temporal, to the invisible by the visible—from the created and human to the divine and uncreated. In the Old Testament he wins his people's trust by giving them what they want, so that in the New Testament they may trust him to give what they truly need.

From the divine economy and the divine pedagogy—from what the Scriptures show us of God's plans and methods—we come to understand who God is.

The God revealed in Scripture is a covenant God, a Father who punctuates salvation history with covenants, making men and women not only his creatures, but in his own image and likeness, his sons and daughters. The God revealed in Scripture is a Father who stoops down to his children and lifts them up to share in his blessings.

Finally, in the New Covenant God fully reveals himself as a Trinity, a Trinity that in its heart is family, an eternal family whose life-giving love is the ultimate source of the *economy*, of salvation history, and of our sacramental liturgy and covenant communion.

::

God's plan was revealed in Christ not for our information, but for our salvation—for the salvation of the world.

The Word was meant to be learned, yes, and studied

and interpreted. But it is a dead letter if we stop there. The Word was meant to be heard, proclaimed, shouted from the rooftops. Our interpretation of Scripture has to be lived and prayed and preached, so that the meaning of the Holy Writ is writ large not only in the hearts and minds of Christians, but in the hearts and minds of their neighbors as well. Written text must become living Word, creating new lives out of the shell of old, re-creating men and women in light of the mystery of Christ revealed in the Word of God.

Jesus never told his Church to publish a book and get people to read it.

How can anybody understand the divine mysteries Scripture contains unless someone guides them (see Acts 8:30–31; Romans 10:14–15)? People need a guide, and the Church is that guide, entrusted with the key to Scriptures and promised the Spirit of truth to lead her and teach her in all things (see John 14:26; 16:12–14). That is why after teaching his Apostles the interpretation of Scripture, Jesus sent them out to be his witnesses: "Go...preach... baptize..." Through their preaching and interpretation of the Word, they were to lead men and women to baptism, to the sacraments of the New Testament.

When he opened up the Scriptures for his disciples, their hearts burned within them. When they, in turn, interpreted the Scriptures, the people who heard their preaching were "cut to the heart" (Acts 2:37, see also Hebrews 4:12). That should be the goal of all study of the sacred page—to be able to live it and proclaim it as life-changing reality, to cleave hearts asunder and set hearts ablaze. Christians have to "actualize" the Scriptures, to make them come alive so that they become a crossroads, a turning point in the lives of all who hear and read them.

"What must we do?" they cried when they heard Peter's interpretation of the Scriptures. "What is to prevent my being baptized?" the Ethiopian cried when Philip opened the Scriptures to him (Acts 2:37; 8:37). That is the reaction we are looking for when we preach, when we interpret, when we study the Word. The Word proclaimed should lead to conversion, to entry into the sacramental liturgy, especially the Eucharist, where the power of the Word to transform is experienced in all its fullness.

The Church's liturgy is the consummation of the divine economy revealed by the Apostles' own reading of Scripture. All of salvation history can be seen as leading to the liturgy, to the sacraments. Some years ago, the great scholar and churchman Jean Daniélou observed:

> Thus we have brought out the traditional teaching. The sacraments are conceived in relation to the acts of God in the Old Testament and the New. God acts in the world; His actions are the *mirabilia*, the deeds that are his alone. God creates, judges, makes a covenant, is present, makes holy, delivers. These same acts are carried out in the different phases of the history of salvation. There is, then, a fundamental analogy

between these actions. The sacraments are simply the continuation in the era of the Church of God's acts in the Old Testament and the New. This is the proper significance of the relationship between the Bible and the liturgy. The Bible is a sacred history; the liturgy is a sacred history.

He makes many important distinctions. Sacraments are not human acts. As Saint John Chrysostom once said of the Mass: Nothing merely human happens there. Sacraments are not what human beings do for God, but what God does for human beings. They are not automatic, magical, or mechanical, but they are indeed powerful.

The Lutheran scholar Oscar Cullmann saw the sacraments as the fulfillment of not only the Old Testament types, but also the New Testament miracles, which were real events, but also (and *primarily*) signs of the sacraments to come. The sacraments "take the place... of the miracles performed by the incarnate Christ."

It may seem startling when we read claims like this in modern scholars such as Cullmann, but it is not a new discovery. It is rather a *recovery* of the methods of the early Fathers and New Testament writers—and indeed Jesus himself. The Greek Fathers, following Saint Paul, called the sacraments "the mysteries," and they are indeed the fulfillment of all the successive covenants in the "mysterious plan of God." The Church and her Apostles, and in turn their successors, serve as "stewards of the mysteries of God" (I Corinthians 4:I).

The early Christians explained the sacraments by means of a method they called *mystagogy,* an initiation into the divine mysteries, the hidden plan of the saving work of Christ. Mystagogy moves a Christian's awareness from the visible to the invisible, from the temporal to the eternal, from the human to the divine, from the earthly to the heavenly, from the sacraments to the mysteries. Typology shows us how Christ fulfills the Old Covenant; mystagogy shows us how Christ sends the Spirit to extend his fulfillment to us, to bring us into his New Covenant.

The Body of Christ that is risen and ascended in glory *is* the New Covenant; and it radiates out through the Spirit to encompass each one of us—through the liturgy and the sacraments.

God's special presence is no longer limited to the Temple, as it had been in the Old Testament. His presence is now manifest in the person of Christ. He is truly present in the sacraments, which fulfill the Old Testament types as well as the New Testament miracles. The types and the miracles, again, were real historical events, but also "signs" of the "greater works" the Apostles would do in the Church (see John 14:12). They were signs of the sacraments, which now bring Christ's glory to the world.

Through mystagogy Christians come to understand that salvation history did not end with the ascension of

Christ, but continues in the mission of the Spirit in the Church, in the sacred liturgy, where the Word becomes action, a "saving actualization" where the fruits of his Passion and Resurrection are truly given to each of us. This vision is clear in all the writings of the post-Ascension Church, from Acts and the Epistles through the book of Revelation and the works of all the Church Fathers. Christ glorified in heaven is active in history on earth, in cosmic history, but also all our personal histories. Through the Word enacted in the sacraments, he has acted in our lives. As the *Catechism* says, in the liturgy of the New Covenant, the Church reveals the fulfillment of the divine economy of salvation and gives us the power, the grace to share in it, to live it.

In effect, the sacraments bring us into that history, make each of our lives an event in that salvation history. In mystagogy we see how the great interventions of God in salvation history, the marvels of God—the creation, the waters of the flood, the crossing of the Red Sea, and the like—were signs of how God would extend his covenant promises to each of us in the sacraments. By his Word spoken in the Spirit, the Father brought forth living things from the waters at the creation of the world; and now he does the same thing for us in baptism, giving us new birth, making each of us by grace a new creation.

Typology shows us a God who is covenant. He binds himself to creation by his Word just as he brings creation into existence by his Word. He is a Father who through covenants brings about a sacred bond of kinship and communion between himself and his children. Daniélou demonstrates this beautifully:

> The covenant is the act by which God promises, in an irrevocable way, to establish communion of life between man and himself. Christ realizes the new and eternal covenant... We should not forget the fact that *'the Covenant' was one of our Lord's names in primitive Christianity, following the text of Isaiah: 'I have made you: Covenant of the peoples' [Isaiah 42:6].* Baptism is our introduction into this covenant. Baptism establishes it by the pledge of God and that of man... And... as the covenant is our bond with God, it is also our incorporation in the people of God.

Mystagogy helps us understand that the sacraments are covenant oaths, through which God binds himself to each of us personally in his New Covenant, his New Testament.

In the covenants of old, God's promise, his pledge of himself, has to be matched by an act of faith, a pledge of fidelity, a covenantal oath sacrifice. It is no different in the New Covenant. We must respond to the covenant offered in Christ with a pledge of "the obedience of faith" (Romans 1:5; 16:26). We do that in the sacramental liturgy. We swear an oath, give our consent, and pledge to give ourselves to him, to become heirs of his covenant promises, children in the family of God.

The covenantal essence of the sacraments—especially baptism and the Eucharist—was explicit in the early liturgies and mystagogy. We need to recover that understanding again. We need to recover our sense of the saving power of the Word of God and the response of faith he seeks from us in the liturgy.

∷

From all this, it should be clear that the liturgy is far from merely symbolic ritual. There is no greater realism than sacramental realism. The sacraments are a direct continuation in our lives of the creative, redemptive, and revelatory action of the Eternal Word, the Word made flesh in Jesus, the Word inspired in the sacred Scripture. This is why Saint Peter could describe the newly baptized as "born anew...through the living and abiding Word of God" (1 Peter 1:23).

God's Word is always an enactment, a new creation. When God says, "Let there be..." he is not *describing* things; he is *fashioning* what is to be. When he says, "I will make my covenant with you...you shall be my people...," he is creating a people where once there was no people (see 1 Peter 2:10).

In the liturgy too by the power of the Spirit, words become acts, speech becomes the creative utterance of the Almighty Trinity. The words illuminate the mysteries, actualize them, make them present, deliver the promises they bespeak. It is not our words that do this, but *God's Word*, made alive in the Holy Spirit. When the priest says, using the words of Christ, "This is my body," at the height of the Mass, he is not just saying something. He is *doing* something—doing what Christ commanded when he said, "Do this." He is giving to those of us kneeling on the other side of the altar something that was not there before he said those words.

The same is true for all of the sacraments: "I baptize you," "I absolve you…" Saint Augustine said the Word, spoken through the medium or minister of the Church, transforms the elements of the sacrament—bringing to the water in baptism, for instance, its saving power. As Christ promised, the Word of the priests is not his own, but the Word of the one who sent him (Luke 10:16).

We speak of the Scriptures as having dual authorship, human and divine, the Holy Spirit cooperating with human writers. In a similar way, the sacramental liturgy involves a "dual agency"—the Word of Christ is spoken in the Spirit by the human minister. This is the great sacramental vision of the Church. It flows directly from our belief in the power of the Word of God and in the economy and pedagogy—the plan and the methods—by which God works through human collaborators to reveal his divine truths to us, and gives us his grace and Spirit.

CHAPTER 13

✣

The Sacramentality of Scripture

Though we are keenly aware of Scripture's use of symbols, metaphors, analogies, and literary devices, the Catholic approach to biblical interpretation is, first and foremost, literal and historical. As the medieval theologian Hugh of Saint Victor said: "*Historia fundamentum est.*" History is fundamental. It is the foundation.

We do not have access to the truth about biblical history without the words of the Scripture. *Dei Verbum,* the Second Vatican Council's Constitution on Divine Revelation, refers to the "inner unity" of words and deeds in history. It is God who speaks and acts. God's speech interprets what he has done so that we understand the meaning of his action.

Why has God done the things that he has done in history? One word: Love. In Deuteronomy 4, Moses summarized the whole history of God's dealings with mankind, and with Israel in particular, by saying that everything was done "because he loved your fathers and chose their descendants after them."

God does what he does and says what he says in history because he loves. It is more than words and propositions. Love requires that inner unity of word and deed. It is the integrity of the divine self-gift that really validates the truth of his love as he has expressed it in history.

This is an understanding that we take into our reading of the Bible even when we begin with the seemingly mundane action of trying to understand the literal meaning of a text.

We have to remember, first and foremost, that the Bible is the product of both God and the human authors. This is a point that fundamentalists miss: God is the principal author of Scripture, but the human authors are no less authors. The mystery of the divine inspiration does not dispense with human authorship, so we cannot dispense with hard literary analysis. We have to go back and see that the human writers are, themselves, true authors.

We apply the classical literary tools, analyzing how the human authors of Scripture used grammar, logic, and rhetoric. Grammar looks at the meaning of words and combinations of words. Logic looks at the truth that is conveyed by those words when they are combined in sentences. Rhetoric looks at how the persuasive power is effected so that the meaning of words is delivered in a way that is convincing and persuasive.

In doing this, we avoid "literalism." While we analyze grammar, logic, and rhetoric, we also look for the figurative. We identify figures of speech, literary devices, metaphors, simile, synechdoche—all the techniques that enhance human speech and make communication something very human. We're never in a rush to get beyond the literal. We see how the words of the text signify things at many, many different levels.

But we also recognize that the *letter* is a *sign*—that the letter, the word, the sentence, the paragraph, the book is itself a set of signs and that the thing signified is a truth of history. Not all "truths" are historical events, of course. The ethical admonitions conveyed in the Letter of Saint James aren't "events," because the Epistle does not aim to give us a historical narrative. Nevertheless to understand the ethical truths that the letter conveys requires us to understand the historical context of the first-century Church.

We have to do the same kind of historical analysis whenever we try to identify literary forms, such as parable, song, or poetry, or when we try to identify literary figures and devices. Ultimately, we want to see how the literary sense of the text conveys historical truth—either the truth of an event, such as the crucifixion, or the truth of a created reality such as water, light, mountains, trees, or the way the text conveys ethical and other truths about human nature. We always situate the literary sense within a historical context.

Just as we have to understand the literary in terms of the grammatical, the logical, and the rhetorical, so we have to understand the historical in terms of time, culture, and religion. In terms of time, we have to understand the period and the events that took place within that period. We have to look at the culture in order to capture the historical background, the customs, and so forth. But with the Bible, we cannot stop at the historical and the cultural as we can in reading other books. To understand the literal words of the texts in their historical and cultural context, we examine the religious understanding—what the authors of the Bible and their audience brought to the text.

In other words: Whether you believe that God is speaking in Scripture or not, you are not going to understand fully what the human writers intended to convey unless you read their writings *on their own terms*—and their own terms are inescapably religious.

An example: When you see the word "Temple" in Scripture, you cannot simply think of a large building with a dome where people go to pray. The literary sign "temple" for the biblical writer conveys far more than the historical reality of a sacred architecture. The Temple for ancient Israel was the central bank as well as the central sanctuary; it was the place of divine government as well as the place of divine worship. It was the place where you got credit as well as where you received the creed. It was Wall Street, the White House, Oxford, and the Vatican all rolled into one.

If you stop at the historical and the literary reading of the texts and do not attend to the religious meaning, you will miss the basic literal meaning of all sorts of Scripture passages.

So we study the literary sense, which gives us the historical truth of events, ideas, and concepts; and the integral meaning of these events, ideas, and concepts is religious.

To read the Bible in the terms in which it is written, we have to debunk the modern notion that religion is something individualized, private.

For the writers of the Bible, as for many of the inhabitants of the classical world, life was essentially religious. Cicero understood this in ancient Rome. For him, *religio*, "religion," was a natural virtue, the "virtue of virtues," the only virtue that could unite and integrate all of human life—the interior and the exterior, the personal and the social, the private and the public.

In ancient Israel, too, we find this understanding of the essentially religious meaning of life. When we read the Bible, then, we are reading the words of people who were trying to convey, through literary means, historical truths that impart the religious meaning of human life. History for the writers of the Bible makes no sense apart from God.

The "literal" meaning of the biblical books, then, is that Israel's victories and successes, its defeats and exile, its captivity and deliverance—its entire history—has a religious meaning. But this religious meaning was not something that the biblical writers "read into" the history of Israel. Understanding the biblical writers on their own terms, we have to acknowledge that they believed that God was both the beginning and the end of all history, and that without reference to God's words and deeds you cannot really understand the integral meaning of what has happened or is happening. You cannot understand the goal, the purpose toward which all of those historical events and processes are directed.

We think about the mystery of the inspiration of Scripture in similar terms. Just as the divine and human interpenetrate in history without diminishing human freedom, so divine inspiration does not diminish the freedom of Scripture's human authors.

This way of thinking flows directly from the mystery of the Incarnation. The mystery of the Word Incarnate is the fact that Christ is fully human, body and soul. He experienced human bodily life at every level—the five senses, the human emotions, and all the rest. At the same time he experienced human life at the psychological level of the soul, the intellect, and the will. This truly human experience was not diminished by his divinity, but was enhanced. Being divine did not make him less human; it made him capable of experiencing everything human to the fullest degree.

In a similar way, the human writers were enhanced by

the gift they received from the Holy Spirit, even though they might not have been conscious of it. Since nothing human is alien to Christ except sin, there is nothing human that is alien to Scripture except error.

In the inspiration of Scripture, we see grace building upon nature. More than that, we see the deepest desires of human nature being fulfilled by grace in a way that surpasses the limits of all natural human longing. That is something beautiful: Grace not only satisfies and fulfills our longings; it transcends them to an infinite extent. In a certain sense, we can say that grace gives us "What no eye has seen, nor ear heard, nor the heart of man conceived" (1 Corinthians 2:9).

We have to respect the mystery of inspiration when we go about the task of reading and interpreting the Bible. We need to have *faith* in what the writers themselves say: for they wish to convey not their own personal take on matters, but the divine perspective. Faith does not abolish reason or replace it. Faith builds upon reason as grace builds upon nature. Faith presupposes reason and builds upon it for the purpose of healing the defects of sin and error, of perfecting it so that it can reason most reasonably—so that we can actually reason about things that reason could never know or demonstrate on its own.

At this level, the task of interpretation is taken up and enveloped in a spiritual grace—a charism of inspiration. Divine inspiration does not simply end with the death of the last biblical author. True, inspiration *as inspiration* is a property that is only attributed to the authors of Scripture. But inasmuch as the Church is animated by the same Spirit who was the inspirator of the biblical writers, in the Church's liturgy and in its dogmas and doctrines we find that the literary sense and historical truths of the Scripture reveal the religious meaning of salvation history, which is ongoing.

When we read the Scriptures "in the Spirit in which they were written," as the Church tells us we must, their religious meaning grows deeper and larger. We find ourselves standing in the middle of a stream of salvation history, as Ezekiel was (see Ezekiel 47): the water starts at ankle-deep, then rises to knee-deep and then waist-deep. Eventually, it is too deep to sound the depths. That is what the interpreter finds when he or she is reading the literal sense and the historical truth of the biblical text, seeking the religious and theological meaning.

When we read with this faith, the religious meaning of history is picked up and elevated through the Holy Spirit. We see that the human writers of Scripture used words to convey the truth of what God is doing in history. We see that, as the *Catechism* says, the words of Scripture are signs and that the events and realities signified by those words are themselves signs and mysteries.

Tradition tells of the "spiritual senses" of Scripture, which build upon the literal and historical senses—not like oil upon water, but like water becoming wine. A transformative process takes place. The spiritual sense transforms the literary and historical meaning of the text. Wine retains certain common elements and characteristics with water, but it is something greater than water. In the same way, the spiritual senses give us a metaphysical realism, a realism that embraces the historical, but rises above it, giving us a much greater meaning.

So when John 2 tells us that Jesus is the fulfillment of all that the Old Testament promised the Temple to be, we understand that Jesus is something infinitely greater than the Temple. And we understand that Christ's fulfillment of the Temple does not terminate with him or his body. Christ extends his fulfillment of the Temple—through the Church—to each Christian. So the Church is the Temple, as Paul says in 1 Corinthians 3, and each one of us is a temple, as he says in 1 Corinthians 6.

The spiritual reading of Scripture enables us to understand that what is true in the state of grace on earth is amplified and infinitely fulfilled in the state of glory in heaven. In Revelation, the New Jerusalem is shaped like the Holy of Holies in the original Temple at Jerusalem. The Holy of Holies on earth was unapproachable, yet it is what all of us will possess forever in the perfect Temple of the celestial Jerusalem.

The serious student of the Bible should want it all and be optimistic about the possibilities of understanding the Scripture in its literal and spiritual senses. We can grow through our efforts—our study, contemplation, prayer—and whatever we accomplish God will crown through his graces. When he does, he will simply be completing what he himself has begun. For the desire to know the Scriptures is itself his grace.

Readers of the Bible should be like Ezekiel in the Old Testament and John the Seer in the New. We need to "eat" the sacred texts—consume them—make them part of us. We have to assimilate the Word as food. We have to find the bread of life in Scripture just as we find it in the Eucharist.

The Second Vatican Council emphasized that these should not be separate or unrelated actions: "The Church has always venerated the divine Scriptures just as she venerates the body of the Lord, since, especially in the sacred liturgy, she unceasingly receives and offers to the faithful the bread of life from the table both of God's word and of Christ's body." And since the council this has been a recurring theme in the Church's magisterium. Very early in his pontificate, Pope John Paul II reminded a great crowd at Jasna Gora, Poland: "the Fathers of the Church have described in an expressive and symbolic way, two tables: one of the Word of God, the other of the Eucharist. The work that we take on ourselves consists in approaching these two tables in order to be filled."

Pope Benedict XVI emphasized that the document is ordered to the sacrament. The word of life leads us to the bread of life: "'from the two tables of the Word of God and the Body of Christ, the Church receives and gives to the faithful the bread of life.' Consequently it must constantly be kept in mind that the word of God, read and proclaimed by the Church in the liturgy, leads to the Eucharist as to its own connatural end."

✛

CHAPTER 14

The Testament at the Heart of the Church

nother favorite theme of the recent popes is the "heart of the Church." They speak of hymns of praise rising from the heart of the Church (*ex corde ecclesiae*), saints emerging from there, and universities being born from there.

How do we read the Bible "from the heart of the Church"? The phrase can have many meanings, all of them instructive. It suggests the dispositions we should have when we approach the Scriptures. We are trusting children of our Father God and of the Church, our mother. We read the sacred page within a community that's larger than our local Bible-study group. Our on-going "study group" is the Communion of Saints, the voices of Catholic Tradition, the great cloud of witnesses from all of history, who continue to intercede on our behalf. Our guide is the Holy Spirit, working through the Church's magisterium.

Most important, we should read the Bible in its natural and supernatural habitat. We should read the Bible in light of the liturgy.

The Bible and the liturgy were made for each other. That statement would have seemed self-evident to the Apostles and the Church Fathers. There were no printing presses in their day, and very few people could afford to have books copied out by hand. So people did not so much read the Scriptures as absorb them, mostly in the Mass. Together, the *document* and the *sacrament* constituted the *Testament*. Moreover, the Mass itself is a stunning compendium of scriptural texts, and it has always included extended readings from the Old and New Covenants.

In the early Church, the Bible was considered a liturgical book. Indeed, the canon—the official "list" of books in the Bible—was originally drawn up to limit the texts that could be used as readings in the Mass.

But the connection goes back even further than that. For the scriptural texts themselves presume the context of the Mass. The Apostles and evangelists seem to be writing with liturgical proclamation in mind.

If we read the New Testament as they wrote it, we'll read it from the heart of the Church. And that heart is Eucharistic. It is the heart of Jesus.

::

The Mass is the one thing that Catholics experience on a weekly basis all their lives, and the Bible is the one book that they will hear at every Mass. Since Masses on Sundays and holy days usually include three readings from the two testaments, plus a fourth from the Book of Psalms, the average faithful Catholic spends about fifteen hours a year in focused Bible study. If you include the other overtly biblical parts of the Mass (the "Holy, Holy, Holy," the "Lamb of God," the "Lord, Have Mercy," and so on), the average time per annum doubles or triples. For the Catholic who goes to daily Mass, the totals are quite impressive, rivaling even the hours spent by some scholars.

Scholars have written mighty tomes, and saints have spent long lives, teaching people what it means to study the Bible faithfully. Here we'll offer just a brief word on interpretation—three short principles, actually, which were decreed by the Second Vatican Council in its Dogmatic Constitution on Divine Revelation, *Dei Verbum*. These "criteria" were summarized in the *Catechism of the Catholic Church* in the following form:

- *"Be expecially attentive 'to the content and unity of the whole Scripture'"* (CCC 112);
- *"Read the Scripture within 'the living Tradition of the whole Church'"* (CCC 113);
- *"Be attentive to the analogy of faith"* (CCC 114).

The Church's first criterion protects us from wrenching verses out of context, making them out to mean something other than what their divine and human authors intended. The true context of every verse in the Bible consists of the words and paragraphs that surround it—the book in which it appears. The true context is the book of the Bible, but also *the book that is the Bible*. The complete literary context of any Scripture verse includes all the books from Genesis to Revelation, because the Bible is a unified book, not merely a library of different books.

The second criterion places the Bible firmly within the context of a community that treasures a "living tradition." That community is the Communion of Saints. We test our own interpretations, measuring them against the tradition of interpreters who have gone before us. We believe that our ancestors have much to teach us. They should have a vote. This approach protects us from the ever-present arrogance that believes we have just now reached the pinnacle of human knowledge and insight. Catholics should have the humility to learn from the past, and to know that the tradition is still *living* today, in the preaching of the saints and the teachings of the Church. Scholarly fads will come and go. The truth abides, unchanging.

The third criterion leads us to examine scriptural texts within the framework of the fullness of Catholic faith. If we believe that the Scriptures are divinely inspired, we must also believe them to be internally coherent and consistent with all Catholic doctrine. The Church's dogmas are not something added to Scripture. Remember: Dogmas are simply the Church's interpretation of Scripture.

Pope Benedict XVI spoke of these three criteria in his 2010 apostolic exhortation *Verbum Domini* (the Word of the Lord), which is arguably the most important document on Scripture produced by the Church in many years.

In the same letter, the pope brought the Church back to its beginnings as he said: "A faith-filled understanding of sacred Scripture must always refer back to the liturgy." In other words: We cannot make sense of the New Testament document without recourse to the New Testament sacrament. It's good for us to study the Bible at home and in our groups, and even at university or seminary if we're called and inclined that way, but all this will find its earthly completion only in our faithful participation in the Mass.

Pope Benedict made so bold a statement about this relationship that I must quote it at length:

> Word and Eucharist are so deeply bound together that we cannot understand one without the other: the word of God sacramentally takes flesh in the event of the Eucharist. The Eucharist opens us to an understanding of Scripture, just as Scripture for its part illumines and explains the mystery of the Eucharist. Unless we acknowledge the Lord's real presence in the Eucharist, our understanding of Scripture remains imperfect.

The Bible is not merely informative, the Holy Father went on to say, but "performative." It leads us to an action: the Eucharist, which Jesus meant to be transformative.

Though the Bible can and should be studied, it is, first and foremost, to be proclaimed and interpreted in the context of liturgical worship. The Bible is at home in the Church, and especially at Mass, where we encounter it in its richness and we ponder it in the homily and in our prayer. "The primary setting for scriptural interpretation," said the pope, "is the life of the Church."

The Catholic Tradition would have us focus not simply on words, but on the Word. For it is the person of Jesus who is the fullness of God's revelation. And that revelation, "the Word became flesh," precedes and exceeds the words of Scripture. God's Word comes to us in creation, in sacred Tradition, and in a symphony of other ways.

Still, only Scripture gives us the Word of God in human words. Scripture speaks the Word, Pope Benedict said, "in an altogether singular way." From cover to cover, Testament to Testament, the Bible is about the Word of God. What unites the Bible's words is that they are all about the Word. As Saint Augustine put it: "Remember that one alone is the discourse of God which unfolds in all sacred Scripture, and one alone is the word which resounds on the lips of all the holy writers." There may be two Testaments, dozens of books, and many thousands of words—but the Bible is one.

The Holy Father reached back to the Church Fathers

to retrieve an idea whose time has come again. Jesus is indeed "the Word," but for our sake God has "abbreviated" his Word: "the eternal word became small—small enough to fit into a manger. He became a child, so that the word could be grasped by us." Benedict obviously delighted in this idea of "abbreviation," which he traced back to the Fathers of the third century and beyond, to Saint Paul and even the prophet Isaiah.

The Incarnation shows the extent of God's love for us. God so loved the world that he gave us his only Son and accommodated himself to our human form—thus enabling us to be accommodated to his form! He wants us to live as his children and partake of his divine nature (see 2 Peter 1:4 and 2 Corinthians 8:9).

That in itself is nothing less than salvation, nothing less than the Gospel, nothing less than the New Testament.

CHAPTER 15

✠

Coming Full Circle

I t's an old, old story.

In the fourth century, in North Africa, lived a brilliant young professor of rhetoric named Augustine. Augustine's career as a scholar proceeded from glory to glory, but he treated his work as something distinct and even separate from his study of the Bible. Indeed, he was first drawn to biblical studies as a teenager, turning to Holy Writ in his generalized search for truth. He was put off, however, by the inelegant language and barbarous behavior he found in the Old Testament, so he turned instead to the more trendy schools of thought: the Manicheans and Neoplatonists, who promised a doctrine demonstrable by reason alone. It was among them that he spent his entire academic career, taking teaching posts in Carthage, Rome, and finally the empire's administrative center in Milan.

It was there that he encountered the Bible again—as

if for the first time—in the liturgical preaching of Saint Ambrose of Milan. It was in Milan, at Mass, that he experienced the Bible in its natural and supernatural setting, proclaimed and preached by a holy bishop. "Every Sunday," he wrote, "I listened as he preached the word of truth to the people, and I grew more and more certain that it was possible to unravel the tangle woven by those who had deceived both me and others with their cunning lies against the Holy Scriptures."

Remember, now, that we are talking about one of the greatest intellects of the fourth century—and indeed one of the leading lights in all intellectual history. Yet he found the grace of understanding not in the stacks of a research library, or at the desk in his study, but in the nave of a cathedral, where he stood among shopkeepers and fishmongers, seamstresses and beggars—all equally dependent on the salvific grace of the New Testament, given in the Church's liturgy, and given through the preaching of a *bishop*, a successor of the Apostles. Ambrose opened the Old Testament for Augustine by interpreting it typologically—according to the tradition of the Church—showing that it foreshadowed a fulfillment in the New Testament.

Augustine was stirred to pray to God: "You made me understand that I ought not to find fault with those who believed your Bible, which you have established with such great authority amongst almost all the nations of the earth, but with those who did not believe; and that I ought to pay no attention to people who asked me how I could be sure that the Scriptures were delivered to mankind by the Spirit of the one true God who can tell no lie. It was precisely this that I most needed to believe."

For Augustine, the move toward Scripture was a decisive move away from his former philosophical positions. To mark his change of heart and mind, he composed an autobiographical dialogue that he titled *Contra Academicos*. Decades later, he would summarize that work and that period in his life: "I purposed by the most cogent reasoning I could muster to rid my mind of the arguments of the academics. For they cause many to despair of finding truth and prevent the wise man from assenting to anything or granting anything at all as clear and manifest, since to them everything appears obscure and uncertain. These arguments were troubling me also. Through the Lord's mercy and help I succeeded in my design."

Augustine intended his dialogue to be historically accurate. Yet modern interpreters believe he was also indulging in allegory when he related some of the incidental details of his drama.

Twice in that work, Augustine's dialogue with his colleagues is interrupted as his mother, Monica (in the text "our mother"), urges the debaters to "come in to eat... lunch is ready." The reader gets the sense that, for Augustine, truth is to be found not in endless discussion, but at the table of Mother Church.

It is there indeed—at the altar, in the liturgy—that Augustine encountered sound and satisfying exegesis in the preaching of Ambrose. It is there that he gained the insight he had failed to gain in his private study, public schooling, and restless inquiry. Pope Benedict put the matter succinctly in his apostolic exhortation *Verbum Domini* (29): *"The primary setting for scriptural interpretation is the life of the Church."*

Augustine was never alone at that altar, for in the liturgy he knew the company of all the saints and angels of heaven, as well as the citizens of the earth, in their stunning variety. So many were drawn to the altar by the story of the covenant, told in the Testaments, but manifest in power through the sacraments. The saints were not ashamed to acknowledge that the Scriptures lacked the fine diction of Seneca or the rhetoric of Cicero. But in a court of law, eloquence was no guarantee of acquittal. In the Church, however, the contrition expressed in the Psalms could not fail to win God's mercy.

As for the passages which had previously struck me as absurd, now that I had heard reasonable explanations of many of them I regarded them as of the nature of profound mysteries; and it seemed to me all the more right that the authority of Scripture should be respected and accepted with purest faith, because while all can read it with ease, it also has a deeper meaning in which its great secrets are locked away. Its plain language and simple style make it accessible to everyone, and yet it absorbs the attention of the learned. By this means it gathers all men in the wide sweep of its net … and yet draws so great a throng in the embrace of its holy humility.

That is the embrace that saves, that satisfies, the embrace of the God who exalts us even as he humbles himself.

::

Look again at the Gospel, and look again at the New Testament.

If the Eucharist that Jesus instituted was just a meal, then Calvary was just a Roman execution. But if Jesus instituted the Eucharist to be the Passover of the New Covenant, then it had to involve both sacrifice and communion, as did the Old Covenant Passover.

The words of institution show that Jesus established the Eucharist as the sacrifice of the New Covenant. As such, the Eucharist transformed Calvary from a Roman execution to a holy sacrifice—the consummation of his self-offering that was initiated in the Upper Room. Thus, he didn't lose his life on Good Friday, since he had already given it—in loving sacrifice—on Holy Thursday. Jesus was not the hapless victim of Roman injustice and violence, but rather the willing victim of divine love and mercy.

If Holy Thursday, moreover, is what transforms Good Friday from an execution to a sacrifice, then Easter Sunday is what transforms the sacrifice into a sacrament: Christ's Body is raised in glory, so that it can now be communicated to the faithful. Indeed, it is one and the same sacrifice as what he offered by instituting the Eucharist and then dying on Calvary, only now his sacred humanity is deified *and* deifying, for the life of the world (see John 6:51). This is the high priestly sacrifice that he offers in heaven and on earth.

Through his sacrifice we live a loving relationship with him—with a person, not a book. For he is the covenant. The covenant is the Lord, and not a past event, but an abiding and real presence. If while we are reading the New Testament we do not see that the New Testament is the Eucharist, then we are profoundly misunderstanding the New Testament. Saint Jerome famously said: "Ignorance of Scripture is ignorance of Christ." It is equally true that ignorance of Christ—Christ *really present in the Eucharist*—is ignorance of Scripture.

⠿

Every sacrifice involves an act of faith. To make a holocaust of an ox or a goat was, in the eyes of the world, to accept a permanent loss. Only certifiably insane people do such things voluntarily. Sane people will give up good things if they are compelled to do so, if they believe they'll get something in return, or if love bids them to do so.

The sacrifice of Christ is an act of love. Jesus Christ is God and Lord, and so he lacks nothing. In any event, he could have no realistic earthly expectation of getting anything in return for his death.

His offering in the Upper Room and the sacrifice on

Calvary require an act of faith on our part. Jesus's death looked like anything but fulfillment, anything but triumph, anything but glory. It looked like abject failure—except to eyes of faith.

The Eucharist, in turn, follows the pattern of Christ's offering, which is the pattern of his suffering. It looks to all the world like a wafer and a sip of inexpensive wine. Yet we call it by the most exalted names. We call it the *Marriage Supper of the Lamb*, the *eschatological banquet*. We call it *Jesus*. We call it *God*.

Cardinal John Wright was prefect of the Vatican Congregation for the Clergy (1969–1979) and a theologian of great subtlety and wit. An outsize presence and a corpulent man, he knew how to use his size to make a rhetorical point. Once while talking to a group of seminarians he observed, "Why do so many people insist on calling the Mass a banquet?" He paused as he rested his hands on his belly. "It hardly seems a snack to me."

Yes, what looks to the eyes like anything but fulfillment—what tastes to the tongue like anything but glory—is really heaven itself: a covenant new and eternal (Hebrews 13:20–21).

The Word was made flesh, and dwelt among us, and gave his flesh to be our life, Wisdom's Banquet. We live the dream of the prophets and seers, we live the promise of the divine covenant, we are given the bread of angels, whenever we consume the Word.

SOURCES AND REFERENCES

CHAPTER I:
The Sacrament of the Scroll

4   *"signifies the prophets and the apostles. In it the Old Covenant"*: Hippolytus of Rome, Fragment 3, in *Ancient Christian Commentary on Scripture*, Old Testament volume XIII (Downers Grove, IL: InterVarsity Press, 2008), 19.

4   *"Unless we eat the open book first"*: Jerome, *Commentary on Ezekiel* 1.3.1.

4   *"What the Old Testament promised, the New Testament"*: Gregory the Great, *Homiliae in Ezechielem* 1.7.15, quoted in Pope Benedict XVI, Post-Synodal Apostolic Exhortation, *Verbum Domini*, n. 41.

5   *Both men are invited to "take" and "eat"*: See the discussion of these actions in Dom Gregory Dix, *The Shape of the Liturgy* (New York: Seabury, 1982), chapter 4.

6   *"You who are accustomed to attending the divine mysteries*: Origen, *On Exodus* 13.3.

6   *"Thus we grow in the realization, so clear to"*: Pope Benedict XVI, *Verbum Domini*, n. 93; italics in original.

CHAPTER 2:

Before the Book

12   *The practice is not restricted to the canonical books*: See 2 Clement
      2.4; *Barnabas* 4.14; and Polycarp, *To the Philippians* 12.1.

13   *he calls them "the memoirs of the Apostles"*: Saint Justin Martyr,
      First Apology 66; *Dialogue with Trypho* 106.4; see also 103.8,
      and 105.1.

13   *"The Gospels," he says, "could not possibly be"*: Saint Irenaeus,
      Against the Heresies 3.11.8.

14   *He believes that the "collection of Gospels…embodies"*: Larry W.
      Hurtado, "The New Testament in the Second Century:
      Texts, Collections, and Canon," in J. W. Childers and D.
      C. Parker, *Transmission and Reception: New Testament Text-Crit-
      ical and Exegetical Studies* (Piscataway, NJ: Gorgias, 2006),
      24.

14   *"an early and deliberately 'ecumenical' move"*: Ibid.

14   *They belonged not to one or another Christian community*: Saint Ig-
      natius of Antioch, *Letter to the Smyrnaeans* 8.

CHAPTER 3:

The New Testament in the New Testament

17   *In ancient cultures, these words denoted "a widespread legal"*: F. M.
      Cross, *From Epic to Canon: History and Literature in Ancient Israel*
      (Baltimore: Johns Hopkins University Press, 1998), 8.

21   *"In the same way [Jesus] also [took] the cup"*: In the Gospels of
      Matthew and Mark, we find Jesus speaking of the cup as
      containing the "blood of the covenant" (Matthew 26:28
      and Mark 14:24). Significantly, it is the only time the term
      diathēkē appears in those books. Luke follows Paul in using
      the modifier "new" (Luke 22:20).

24   *"How could it ever occur to anyone to interpret the Cross of Jesus"*:
      Joseph Cardinal Ratzinger, *Pilgrim Fellowship of Faith: The*

Church as Communion (San Francisco: Ignatius Press, 2005), 96–97.

25   "the interpretation of Christ's death on the Cross in terms": Ibid., 94–95; italics in original.

25   *"Here, with unique clarity, we encounter* what is specific to the New Testament: Ibid., 73; italics in original.

CHAPTER 4:
The New Testament After the New Testament

28   *Though he never uses the phrase "New Covenant/Testament": Letter of Barnabas,* chapter 4.

28   *Similarly, in the late second century, Saint Melito:* Preserved in Eusebius of Caesarea, *Ecclesiastical History* 4.26.

29   *For Irenaeus, "New Covenant/Testament" refers to:* Saint Irenaeus of Lyons, *Adversus Haereses* 5.33.1.

29   *"Our way of thinking is attuned to the Eucharist":* Ibid., 4.18.5.

29   *Christ "made a New Covenant with us; for what belonged":* Saint Clement of Alexandria, *Stromata* 6.5.

29   *"go and submit himself to the Word as his trainer":* Saint Clement of Alexandria, *Quis Dives Salvetur* 3.

30   *"For this he came down. For this he clothed himself":* Ibid., 37.

30   *"The expressions 'Old Testament' and 'New Testament'":* See Theodore G. Stylianopoulos, *The New Testament: An Orthodox Perspective,* vol. 1, *Scripture, Tradition, Hermeneutics* (Brookline, MA: Holy Cross Orthodox Press, 1997), 26. See also W. C. van Unnik, "He Kaine Diatheke: A Problem in the Early History of the Canon," *Studia Patristica,* IV (1961), 212–27.

31   *At least once he used both terms, instrumentum and testamentum:* See *Against Marcion* 4.1.

31   *He argues against one opponent by using texts:* Tertullian, *Against Praxeas* 15. See also *On Modesty* 1.

31   *The greatest of these, Origen, writing in Greek, routinely used "Old Covenant"*: Origen, *Commentary on John* 5.8.

31   *referred to "the two covenants"*: Saint Hippolytus of Rome, *On Christ and Antichrist* 59.

31   *wrote in Latin of "the Scriptures, old and new"*: Saint Cyprian of Carthage, *Treatise* 12 (*To Quirinius*).

32   *"presumes archaic patterns of thought and behavior"*: George E. Mendenhall, *Ancient Israel's Faith and History: An Introduction to the Bible in Context* (Louisville, KY: Westminster John Knox Press, 2001), pp. 227–29.

33   *He repeatedly calls the Church the* thusiastērion: See Saint Ignatius of Antioch, *Ephesians* 5.2, *Trallians* 7.2, *Philadelphians* 4.

34   *He asserts that the bishop's work is*: 1 Clement 44. On the early dating of this letter, see Thomas J. Herron, *Clement and the Early Church of Rome: On the Dating of Clement's First Epistle to the Corinthians* (Steubenville, OH: St. Paul Center/Emmaus Road, 2008); also, Clayton Jefford, *The Apostolic Fathers and the New Testament* (Peabody, MA: Hendrickson, 2006), 18; J. A. T. Robinson, *Redating the New Testament* (London: SCM, 1976), 327ff.

34   *It is employed by Saint Justin Martyr, Origen*: For these and others, see *Ancient Christian Commentary on Scripture: Old Testament XIV* (Downers Grove, IL: InterVarsity Press, 2003), 288–96.

34   *Recent scholarship suggests that the ritual sections*: On the dating of the liturgical portions of *The Didache*, see Enrico Mazza, *The Origins of the Eucharistic Prayer* (Collegeville, MN: Pueblo, 1995), 40–41; also, Clayton Jefford, *The Apostolic Fathers and the New Testament* (Peabody, MA: Hendrickson, 2006), 20.

34   *"We sacrifice anew, according to the New Covenant"*: Eusebius, *Proof of the Gospel* 1.10.

35   *Around AD 111, the pagan governor of Bithynia*: Pliny, *Letters*
      10.96–97.

36   *Like Saint Paul before him (see 1 Corinthians 8), Saint Cyril contrasts*
      the: Saint Cyril of Jerusalem, *Mystagogical Catecheses* 1.9.

37   *He describes the pacts that had been made with Satan as* diathēkē:
      Ibid., 1.7.

37   *The new Christians had broken those former covenants*: Ibid., 1.9.

CHAPTER 5:

The Original Setting of the New Testament

45   *Over the last fifty years and more, many Protestant biblical scholars*:
      The movement that began with scholars such as Oscar
      Cullmann, F. J. Leenhardt, and Ernst Kasemann contin-
      ues today in the work of John Koenig, Geoffrey Wain-
      wright, and Arthur Just.

46   *In Jesus's own milieu, these terms of "thanksgiving" could refer*: On
      the importance of the *todah* in Second Temple Judaism
      and its influence in nascent Christianity, see Hartmut
      Gese, "The Origin of the Lord's Supper," in *Essays on Bib-*
      lical Theology (Minneapolis: Augsburg Publishing House,
      1981); Harvey H. Guthrie, Jr., *Theology as Thanksgiving* (New
      York: Seabury, 1981); and Jean LaPorte, *Eucharistia in Philo:*
      Studies in the Bible and Early Christianity (New York: Edwin
      Mellen, 1983), 24. A good popular presentation is Tim
      Gray, "From Jewish Passover to Christian Eucharist: The
      Todah Sacrifice as Backdrop for the Last Supper," *Catholic*
      for a Reason III: Scripture and the Mystery of the Mass, eds. Scott
      Hahn and Regis Flaherty (Steubenville, OH: Emmaus
      Road, 2004), 72.

46   *More than a century after the fall of the Temple, the Midrash records*:
      Pesiqta, quoted in Gese, "The Origin of the Lord's Supper,"
      133.

CHAPTER 6:

The Church of the New Testament

50   *In Christianity, he wrote, tradition is "never a simple and anonymous"*: Joseph Cardinal Ratzinger, *God's Word: Scripture, Tradition, Office* (San Francisco: Ignatius Press, 2008), 23.

50   *"The succession is the form of the tradition"*: Ibid., 29.

50   *"[S]uccession is never the taking over of some official powers"*: Ibid., 23.

51   *This process, Ratzinger noted, gives "the living word of proclamation"*: Ibid., 29.

53   *"The Apostles received the gospel for us from the Lord"*: Saint Clement of Rome, *To the Corinthians* 42.

53   *"The Apostles knew…that there would be contention"*: Ibid., 44:1–2.

54   *"I have my refuge in the Gospel and in the flesh of Jesus"*: Saint Ignatius of Antioch, *Letter to the Philadelphians* 5.

54   *"We love the prophets," he said, "because their preaching"*: Ibid.

54   *Saint Ignatius wrote, "I hear some people saying"*: Ibid., 8.2.

55   *"In this order, and by this succession, the ecclesiastical tradition"*: Saint Irenaeus of Lyons, *Against the Heresies* 3.3.2–3.

56   *"It is my purpose to write an account of the successions"*: Eusebius of Caesarea, *Church History* 1.1.1.

CHAPTER 7:

The Old Testament in the New Testament

60   *"First of all you must understand this, that no prophecy"*: See Saint Polycarp, *Letter to the Philippians* 7; Saint Irenaeus, *Against the Heresies* 3.3.4.

62   *"Apostolic writings must have ranked as authoritative writings"*: Richard Bauckham, *Word Biblical Commentary*, vol. 50, *2 Peter, Jude* (Waco, TX: Word, 1983), 333.

62   *"The New Testament is concealed in the Old"*: Saint Augustine of
      Hippo, *Questions on the Heptateuch* 2.73.

64   *"the memoirs of the apostles or the writings of the prophets"*: Saint
      Justin Martyr, *First Apology* 67.

CHAPTER 8:
The Canon of the New Testament

68   *It is known as the Muratorian Canon, and it probably dates*: For a
      complete text of the Muratorian Canon in translation, see
      J. Stevenson (rev. W. H. C. Frend), *A New Eusebius: Docu-
      ments Illustrating the History of the Church to 337 A.D.* (London:
      SPCK, 1987), 123–25. Curiously, the Muratorian Canon
      includes the Old Testament book of Wisdom as a New
      Testament book.

70   *"The effect of their activities is to assist the progress"*: Saint Augus-
      tine of Hippo, *City of God* 16.2; see also 18.51.

70   *Writing in the late third and early fourth centuries, Eusebius employed*:
      Eusebius of Caesarea, *Ecclesiastical History* 3.25.1–7.

72   *"These are the fountains of salvation, that he who thirsts"*: Saint
      Athanasius of Alexandria, *Festal Letters* 39.6.

73   *Larry Hurtado proposes that it is "more correct to see"*: Larry W.
      Hurtado, "The New Testament in the Second Century:
      Texts, Collections, and Canon," in J. W. Childers and D.
      C. Parker, *Transmission and Reception: New Testament Text-Crit-
      ical and Exegetical Studies* (Piscataway, NJ: Gorgias, 2006),
      27; emphasis in original.

74   *In the sixteenth century, Martin Luther expressed his opinion that He-
      brews*: See the discussion of Luther's edition of the New
      Testament in Roland Bainton, *Here I Stand: A Life of Martin
      Luther* (New York: Mentor, 1955), 259–61.

74   *As Pope Pius XI put it in the mid-twentieth century*: Pope Pius XI,
      encyclical letter *Mit Brennender Sorge*.

CHAPTER II:

The New Testament and Christian Doctrine

102   *So swift and sweeping was his success that Saint Jerome*: Saint Jerome, *Dialogue Against the Luciferians* 19.

104   *"Catholic dogma...derives all its content from Scripture"*: Joseph
Ratzinger, "Cardinal Frings's Speeches During the Sec-
ond Vatican Council: Some Reflections Apropos of
Muggeridge's *The Desolate City*," *Communio* 15, no.1 (Spring
1988): 136.

104   *"Dogma is by definition nothing other than an interpretation of Scripture"*: Joseph Ratzinger, "Crisis in Catechetics: Handing
On the Faith and the Sources of the Faith," *Canadian Catholic Review* 7 (June 1983): 178.

105   *"Even if the expressions are not in so many words in the Scriptures"*:
Saint Athanasius of Alexandria, *De Decretis* 21.

105   *And the language of Scripture remains "referential" for the Church*:
Cf. Pontifical Biblical Commission, *Bible and Christology*
(Paulist, 1986): "The 'auxiliary' languages employed in
the Church in the course of the centuries do not enjoy the
same authority, as far as faith is concerned, as the 'refer-
ential language of the inspired authors, especially of the
New Testament with its mode of expression rooted in the
Older [Testament]."

105   *It is true that the Church has been given the Holy Spirit*: See Second
Vatican Council, Dogmatic Constitution on Divine Rev-
elation, *Dei Verbum*, n. 10.

106   *In fact, it empowers us, gives us new powers of insight*: Catechism of the
Catholic Church, nos. 114, 90.

CHAPTER 12:

The Mysterious Plan in the New Testament

107   *Against the Marcionites and Gnostics who rejected the Old Testament*:
       Tertullian, *The Prescription Against Heretics* 36.

107   *The great twentieth-century Dominican Yves Congar said that*: Yves
       Congar, *Tradition and Traditions: The Biblical, Historical, and
       Theological Evidence for Catholic Teaching on Tradition* (Irving,
       TX: Basilica Press, 1998), p. 69.

108   *We find this sense throughout Saint Paul's letters and in the writings of*:
       Saint Ignatius of Antioch, *Letter to the Ephesians* 18.2.

108   *Saint Irenaeus said that "the divine program and economy for the salva-
       tion of humanity"*: Saint Irenaeus of Lyons, *Against the Heresies*
       1.10.3.

109   *With each succeeding covenant, he reveals more fully his intention*:
       On the divine plan, see *Catechism of the Catholic Church*, nos.
       1079–1082.

109   *a worldwide kingdom, a divine family, "a chosen race, a royal priest-
       hood"*: "The Church is nothing other than 'the family of
       God.'" See Ibid., n. 1655; see also nos. 542, 854, 959, 1632;
       and Hebrews 3:6.

110   *it is nothing less than full communion between God and humanity*: See
       Catechism, no. 260: "The ultimate end of the whole divine
       economy is the entry of God's creatures into the perfect
       unity of the Blessed Trinity (cf. John 17:21–23). But even
       now we are called to be a dwelling for the Most Holy
       Trinity: 'If a man loves me,' says the Lord, 'he will keep
       my word, and my Father will love him, and we will come
       to him, and make our home with him' (John 14:23)."

111   *In the third century, the Egyptian scholar Origen said*: Origen, *Frag-
       ment on Deuteronomy* 1.21.

111   *"In the various manifestations of God to man"*: Saint Gregory of
       Nazianzen, *Against Eunomius*. See Stephen D. Benin, *The
       Footprints of God: Divine Accommodation in Jewish and Christian*

Thought (Albany: State University of New York Press, 1993), 52.

112 *"The education of the human race, represented by the people of God"*: Saint Augustine, *City of God* 10.14.

113 *In his accommodation, the Father leads his children to the spiritual*: On the economy and divine condescension and accommodation, see *Catechism*, nos. 53, 56–57, 122, 236, 260, 684, 1093.

115 *"What must we do?" they cried when they heard Peter's interpretation*: Cf. Pontifical Biblical Commission, *Interpreting the Bible in the Church* (Vatican, 1993): IV.C.1: "In principle, the liturgy, and especially the sacramental liturgy, the high point of which is the eucharistic celebration, brings about the most perfect actualization of the biblical texts, for the liturgy places the proclamation in the midst of the community of believers, gathered around Christ so as to draw near to God. Christ is then 'present in His word, since it is He Himself who speaks when holy scriptures are read in the Church' (*Sacrosanctum Concilium*, 7). Written text thus becomes living word."

115 *"Thus we have brought out the traditional teaching"*: Jean Daniélou, S.J., "The Sacraments and the History of Salvation," in *The Liturgy and the Word of God* (Collegeville, MN: Liturgical Press, 1959), pp. 21–32.

116 *The Lutheran scholar Oscar Cullmann saw the sacraments as*: Oscar Cullmann, *Early Christian Worship* (Philadelphia: Westminster, 1978), 118.

117 *The early Christians explained the sacraments by means of a method*: See *Catechism*, nos. 1074–1075.

117 *Typology shows us how Christ fulfills the Old Covenant*: See Enrico Mazza, *Mystagogy: A Theology of Liturgy in the Patristic Age* (Collegeville, MN: Pueblo, 1989).

118 *As the* Catechism *says, in the liturgy of the New Covenant*: "Saving

actualization" is from Daniélou, "The Sacraments and the History of Salvation." See also *Catechism,* nos. 1095, 1104.

119　*"Baptism establishes it by the pledge of God":* Jean Daniélou, S.J., "The Sacraments and the History of Salvation"; emphasis added.

121　*The same is true for all of the sacraments: "I baptize you": Tractates on the Gospel of John* 80, 3 (P.L. 35,1840): "The Word is added to the element, and there results the Sacrament, as if itself also a kind of visible word...For even in the word itself the passing sound is one thing, the abiding efficacy another." Cf. *Catechism,* no. 1228.

CHAPTER 13:
The Sacramentality of Scripture

131　*The Second Vatican Council emphasized that these should not be separate:* Second Vatican Council, Dogmatic Constitution on Divine Revelation, *Dei Verbum,* n. 21.

131　*Very early in his pontificate, Pope John Paul II reminded a great crowd:* Address at Jasna Gora, n. 3, June 3, 1979. He would echo those phrases many times. See, for example, *Mane Nobiscum Domine,* n. 12; *Dominicae Cenae,* n. 10; and his *ad limina* address to the Austrian bishops, November 20, 1998.

131　*Pope Benedict XVI emphasized that the document is ordered to the sacrament:* Pope Benedict XVI, Apostolic Exhortation, *Sacramentum Caritatis* (2007), n. 44.

CHAPTER 14:
The Testament at the Heart of the Church

137　*"Word and Eucharist are so deeply bound together":* Pope Benedict XVI, encyclical letter *Verbum Domini* (2010), n. 55.

138　*The Bible is not merely informative, the Holy Father:* Ibid., n. 53.

138   *"The primary setting for scriptural interpretation"*: Ibid., n. 29.

138   *Scripture speaks the Word, Pope Benedict said*: Ibid., n. 17.

138   *"Remember that one alone is the discourse of God"*: Quoted ibid., n. 18.

139   *"the eternal word became small"*: Ibid., n. 12.

CHAPTER 15:
Coming Full Circle

141   *"Every Sunday," he wrote, "I listened as he preached"*: Saint Augustine, *Confessions* 6.3.

141   *Augustine was stirred to pray to God*: Ibid. 6.5.

142   *"I purposed by the most cogent reasoning I could muster to rid my mind"*: Saint Augustine, *Retractations* 1.1.1.4, quoted in the introduction to John J. O'Meara, ed. and trans., *Against the Academics*, Ancient Christian Writers, vol. 12 (New York: Paulist Press, 1951), 2.

143   *"As for the passages which had previously struck me as absurd"*: Saint Augustine, *Confessions* 6.5.

145   *"Ignorance of Scripture is ignorance of Christ"*: Saint Jerome, *Commentary on Isaiah* 17.